I0816337

BEYOND *the* VEIL

Died 24 Jan. 1805
Aged 18 Months
Blessed Spirit
Rest in Peace.

BEYOND *the* VEIL

THE VICTORIAN OBSESSION WITH DEATH AND MOURNING

Paul Gambino

FRANCES LINCOLN

The well-circulated image by Danish-American journalist, photographer and social reformer Jacob Riis. It shows criminal gangs in one of the city's dangerous areas.

Introduction

To step into the Victorian era of Europe and the United States is to step into a world profoundly and unapologetically steeped in death. Today, we often speak of the topic in hushed tones, as something to be feared or at least avoided in polite conversation, but in the nineteenth century, death was a constant and undeniable presence. It was a guest at every table, lurking in the crowded streets of industrial cities and the lonely country roads, homes filled with children who might not live to see adulthood and even in the grand halls of royalty. For the Victorians, dying was not a distant concept but an intimate companion – often treated with equal parts reverence and fascination.

In *Beyond the Veil: the Victorian Obsession with Dying*, we explore the complex ways in which Victorians embraced death. We assert that this was not only seen as a biological factor of life but that it was woven into the very fabric of Victorian culture and society. But why did both Europeans and Americans of this era transform dying into an elaborate spectacle, creating a death culture that transcended the sombre to enter the realm of the macabre and poetic? To answer these questions, we must look beyond the surface of mourning customs of the time and delve deeper into the physical, psychological and societal forces that shaped the Victorians' relationship with death.

The physical reasons are the easiest to comprehend. The Victorians lived in a world rife with high mortality rates, especially among infants and young children, brutal and unsafe work environments with a large child industrial labour force, a population explosion in major cities that resulted in living conditions that were deplorable and unsanitary. And then there was the crime rate. In nineteenth century Britain, taking a city walk at night was a dangerous endeavour, the streets lined with people of ill-repute, alcoholics and opium addicts, thieves and murderers, the air thick with malodorous air pollution, the streets unsanitary. Ordinary people took their life in their hands each day. Plus, war, outbreaks of disease, such as cholera and influenza, and limited medical knowledge meant that death was classless – even the wealthy could not escape the grim reaper's scythe.

Top: An illustration of a family in complete despair as they live in the London slums (c.1869).
Bottom: An Italian immigrant family living in the tenements of Hull House in Chicago, Illinois.

Life's fragility was impossible to ignore and people sought ways to cope, including trying to instill some order into something beyond human control, and that became mourning, funerals, mourning clothes, and grieving etiquette became increasingly elaborate. Memorial hair art and post mortem photos of loved ones provided comfort to those dealing with loss, a way to remember the dead.

From a psychological perspective, the Victorians' obsession with death can be linked to their deep-seated anxieties about the afterlife. Religion, particularly Christianity, dominated the cultural mindset of the time, and questions of what lay beyond the grave were ever-present. The fear of eternal damnation, coupled with a desire for salvation, led many Victorians to dwell on the idea of a 'good death' – a peaceful passing in the presence of loved ones, with the soul prepared for its journey.

In the chapters that follow we examine death in Victorian times. Chapter 2, In the Shadow of the Scythe, for example, lays the foundation by taking us into the disease-ridden streets of cities of the time. It was here, in these cramped urban spaces, that death showed its most cruel face, taking the young, the weak and sometimes entire families in its grasp. Yet, despite this suffering, life had to carry on. Victorians were resilient and their ability to confront the reality of death through rituals, art and even fashion is a testament to their strength in the face of overwhelming loss.

The monarch embodied everything Victoriana and it is virtually impossible to examine the Victorian obsession with death without referencing Queen Victoria. The untimely passing of her husband, Prince Albert, plunged the queen into a state of deep mourning from which she never truly emerged. Draped in black, the queen's grief became public spectacle, one that rippled across society. Mourning was no longer relegated to the private sphere but became a public duty, one that dictated how the bereaved should behave, dress and even interact with others. For decades, the West watched as the British queen, also figurehead of a huge empire, mourned. Widows and widowers took their inspiration from her, dressing in increasing elaborate mourning costumes, somberly moving through their days. The fashion of mourning became almost as much about status as sorrow. Entire industries thrived off the production of black silk, jet jewellery and veils, turning grief into an aesthetic.

Yet, the Victorians' fascination with death extended far beyond fashion. It infiltrated every sector of society, from medicine, art, architecture to daily

An illustration (c.1890) from a French magazine depicting 'Death stalking a poor family as they sleep in their unsanitary room' in late 19th-century France.

leisure. Nineteenth-century medical knowledge was characterized by a limited understanding of diseases and treatments, leading to often misguided and harmful interventions. Bloodletting, a practice dating back centuries, was still widely employed. Physicians believed in the theory of balancing the body's 'humours' by draining blood, which could weaken patients already suffering from illness. These practices often brought the suffering closer to death's door rather than pulling them back from it.

As graveyards became oversubscribed, a fascination with cemeteries emerged during this time, turning them into ornate and integral parts of daily life, where people would meet, perambulate, even lunch with their dead ones. The epic 'garden cemeteries' like Paris's Père Lachaise and London's Highgate and Kensal Green became veritable outdoor museums adorned with elaborate tombstones, sculptures and manicured gardens. The Magnificent Seven London cemeteries offered people, not just mourners, respite from the crowded, industrial city that surrounded them – as did others around the

Residents of a Victorian-era slum in the infamous Whitechapel area of London.

nation – inviting the living to wander among the dead, while reflecting on mortality and cherishing nature's beauty, these sites fostering a stunning array of flora, fauna and wildlife. Such was the Victorians' fascination with death that the introduction of the Necropolis, which via a dedicated train route linked the city centres to the extensive burial grounds of Surrey's Brookwood Cemetery. Across the Atlantic, the Rural Cemetery Movement created similar spaces.

Regretfully, for some, there was no peace to be found, even in death. With a shortage of cadavers needed by medical schools for anatomical study, grave robbing became a common occurrence and families were forced to take elaborate measures to ensure their deceased loved ones did not end up on the dissection table.

Industrialization brought with it significant societal changes, including the rise of factories and the brutality of factory work life – long hours, dangerous working conditions and factory foremen with little regard for the well-being of their workers. Industrialization dehumanized many aspects of life. People began to feel like mere cogs in a machine, stripped of individuality and autonomy. Advancements in science and technology challenged traditional religious beliefs and raised existential questions, significant social inequality and stark divisions between the wealthy and the impoverished. Literature of the era reflected these anxieties, with authors like Mary Shelley in *Frankenstein*, Bram Stoker in *Drácula* and the ghost stories of Edith Wharton imbued with darkness, cautionary tales about the consequences of human ambition.

Spiritualism also took hold during this era, grieving families seeking to bridge the ever-narrowing gap between the living and the dead. Seances became fashionable events, where mediums claimed to communicate with the deceased, offering solace to those left behind. In a time when death was omnipresent, the hope that the veil between this world and the next could be pierced provided a strange comfort to Victorians.

And if this were not enough, people's imaginations were fuelled by the activities of serial killers such as Jack the Ripper, The Thames Torso Murderer and H.H. Holmes's Murder Castle of Horrors, all splashed across the newspaper headlines. People were fascinated. Death, and brutal death, walked the Victorians' streets.

The art world was not immune to the infinite sadness of the time and grappled with whether to portray death as a beautiful experience or one of

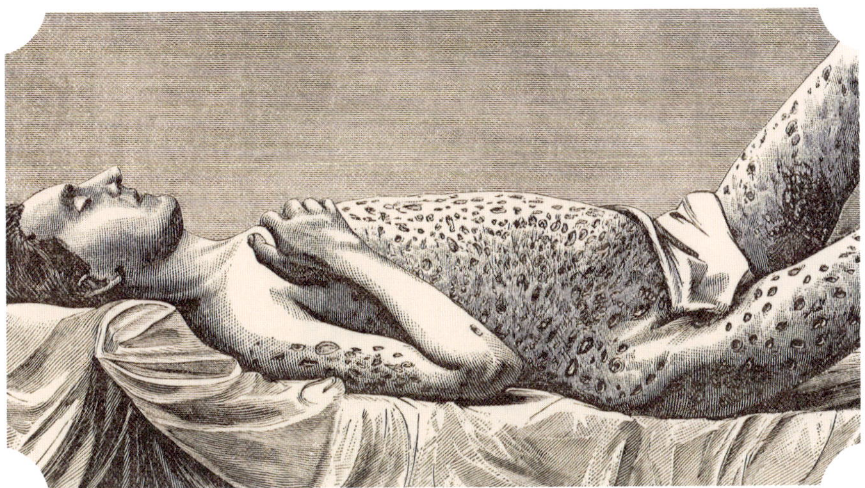

'Result of Subcutaneous Injection' of morphine by hypodermic syringe by addicts.

absolute pain and suffering. A new visual medium came of age at this time: photography. It was becoming accessible to the masses, and with the Victorian obsession, it was inevitable that photographing the dead would become popular, ushering in the elaborate postmortem photographs of the era.

This macabre fascination with death was not a monolithic phenomenon, however. Its impact and importance differed across regions, classes and individuals, influenced by religious beliefs, personal losses and social standing. After our journey together through the next 60 years, hopefully we may have a better understanding of the Victorians' complex relationship with death, and can gain insights into the people of the past and the universal human condition, where life and death are eternally intertwined, each giving meaning to the other.

CHAPTER I

THRONES *and* BONES

THE GRIEF THAT GOVERNS

ASSASSINATIONS, BULLETS AND DEADLY DISEASE

The pain and tragedy felt from death lurking beyond every corner during the Victorian era was present not only by the poor, but all the way up to the highest echelons of power. Presidents, kings, royalty and the children of leaders were not immune to the rampant diseases that claimed countless lives, which were a grim reminder of how status and wealth could not shield them from the harsh reality of death.

Prominent figures suffered just as much as the everyman. An example of this is 9th US President William Henry Harrison, who served the shortest term in American history, succumbing to pneumonia just thirty-one days after his inauguration, in 1841. His death underscored the vulnerability of leaders to common ailments that could quickly turn fatal, due to the limited medical care or knowledge available.

Similarly, 12th US President Zachary Taylor, on 4 July 1850, attended a ceremony at the Washington Monument in Washington, DC to celebrate Independence Day, thus sealing his fate. Following the event, held outdoors in the sweltering summer heat, Taylor reportedly indulged in refreshments, including cherries and iced milk. On his return to the White House, he became violently ill, experiencing severe stomach pain, diarrhoea and vomiting. Initially diagnosed with gastroenteritis, Taylor's condition deteriorated rapidly over the next few days. Despite the best efforts of his physicians, who used the medical practices of the time – including blood-letting and purging (administering vomit inducing substances) – the president died on 9 July 1850, just five days after falling ill. His sudden demise led to Vice-President Millard Fillmore's ascension to the presidency.

In the immediate aftermath of Taylor's death, the official explanation was that he had succumbed to 'cholera morbus', a term used at the time to describe various gastrointestinal illnesses. Like many of the newly industrialized cities, Washington, DC had poor sanitation conditions, and some historians believe that contaminated food or water may have been responsible for his illness.

However, rumours and conspiracy theories began to circulate almost immediately after Taylor's death. Given the political climate of the time, with intense debates over slavery, some speculated that Taylor had been poisoned by pro-slavery advocates. His opposition to the expansion of slavery and his support for California's admission as a free state to the Union made him a controversial figure, and it was not inconceivable that his death was the result of foul play.

The poisoning theory persisted for decades, culminating in an exhumation of Taylor's body in 1991. Historian and author Clara Rising played a pivotal role in this process. While researching a biography of Taylor, Rising became convinced that he might have been poisoned. She speculated that Taylor's death could have been due to arsenic poisoning rather than the commonly believed cause of cholera or gastroenteritis. Through her persistence in challenging historical records and meeting a descendant of Taylor who also questioned his cause of death, Rising convinced his family to allow the exhumation of the president's remains. Tests revealed no significant traces of arsenic, thus ruling out poisoning.[1]

The assassination of James Garfield, 20th President of the United States, marked a tragic episode in American history, not just for the murderous act but for the ensuing medical mismanagement that ultimately led to his death. On 2 July 1881, Garfield was shot by Charles J. Guiteau, a disgruntled office seeker, at the Baltimore and Potomac Railroad Station in Washington, DC. With one bullet grazing his arm and the other lodged in his abdomen, Garfield survived the initial shooting. Dr Willard Bliss, a former American Civil War surgeon with a questionable past – suspected of overcharging patients, profiteering from government contracts during the war, and hawking snake oil cancer cures, and possessing an inflated sense of self-importance – quickly appointed himself as the lead physician, even though Garfield had not requested his services.

Bliss employed aggressive and outdated medical practices that ultimately did more harm than good. At the time, antiseptic techniques were still in their infancy, but Bliss disregarded the evolving understanding of germ theory, which had

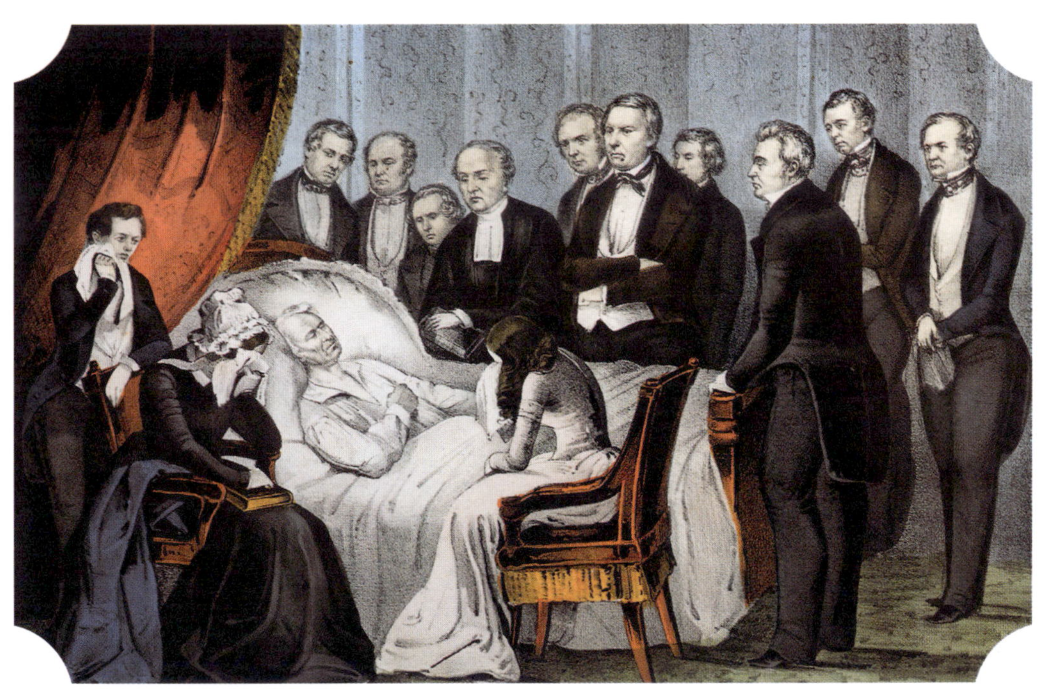

An illustration of the 12th President of the United States, Zachary Taylor, as he lies dying of a case of cholera at the White House surrounded by family and cabinet members.

already been advocated by pioneers like Joseph Lister, a British surgeon who was making great headway using diluted carbolic acid to prevent operative and post-operative infections. Instead, Bliss probed Garfield's wound repeatedly with unsterilized hands and instruments.

Despite the president's initial resilience, his condition deteriorated due to the infection resulting in sepsis and significant pus accumulation in Garfield's body. In a desperate attempt to locate the elusive second bullet, Alexander Graham Bell, the inventor of the telephone, was brought in. Bell developed the induction balance device, an early form of a metal detector, to find the bullet without invasive surgery. Despite multiple attempts, Bell's device initially failed to accurately locate the bullet. This failure was later attributed to interference from the metal bed springs beneath Garfield. On the third attempt, the metal bed springs were removed, but the location of the bullet was still not located. Bliss dismissed Bell's device as useless.

The medical interventions worsened Garfield's condition. Multiple surgeries were performed

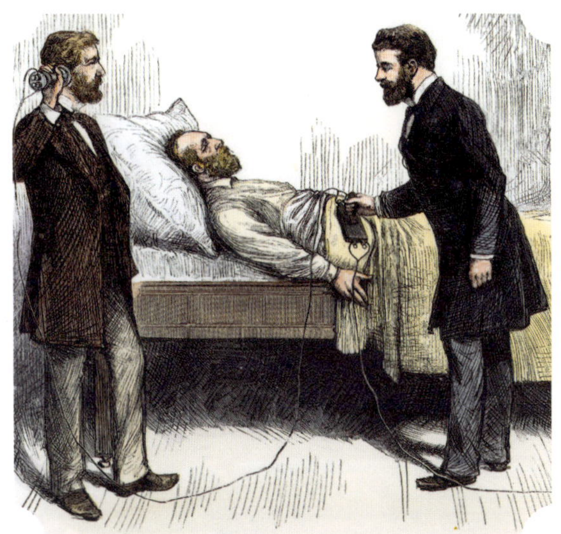

Alexander Graham Bell and Simon Newcomb using induction in an attempt to locate a bullet.

Each invasive procedure introduced more pathogens into the president's body, leading to further deterioration.

in a futile effort to drain the now infected areas and locate the bullet. Each invasive procedure introduced more pathogens into the president's body, leading to further deterioration. He was eventually moved to the Jersey Shore in the hope that his health would improve with fresh air and a more favourable climate. However, this relocation did little to improve his dire condition. He had lost a lot of weight and was weak. The infection, coupled with malnutrition and the physical trauma of the bullet wounds and subsequent surgeries, proved too much for his body.

On 19 September 1881, after enduring months of severe pain and ineffective treatments, President Garfield died from a ruptured splenic artery aneurysm, a complication of the sepsis that ravaged his body.

The aftermath of Garfield's assassination and the botched medical care had significant implications. It accelerated the acceptance of antiseptic methods in the United States, as the medical community and the public now recognized the dangers of infection in surgical and wound treatment. Garfield's death also underscored the importance of improving medical technology and training, leading to future developments that would enhance the accuracy and safety of medical procedures.

In spite of the growing awareness twenty years later, 25th US President William McKinley died in circumstances similar to Garfield's.

A hand-coloured halftone of an illustration of President William McKinley being assassinated by anarchist Leon Czolgosz at Buffalo, New York.

McKinley was assassinated on 6 September 1901, by anarchist Leon Czolgosz, during a public event in Buffalo, New York. Shot twice, initially the gunshot wounds seemed non-lethal, and McKinley showed signs of recovery. However, again, due to poor medical sterilization practices, bacteria likely entered McKinley's body either during the surgery that followed or from his immediate environment, leading to peritonitis – an infection of the abdominal cavity – and eventually gangrene. The infected tissues around his wounds began to decay, cutting off blood flow and causing systemic poisoning. With no antibiotics available at that time, and without proper medical intervention, the spread of infection became irreversible. McKinley's vital organs failed, leading to his death eight days after the shooting.

Death was a frequent visitor to the White House between the years 1845 and 1901. In addition to the death of Harrison, Garfield and McKinley, six other presidents lost fifteen of their young children to disease or accidents. In those sixty years, the men at the helm of the United States were in a relative state of grieving and regret, and the White House was dubbed the 'Black House' by insensitive journalists who commented on the pall of death that seemingly hung over 1600 Pennsylvania Avenue.

THE WHITE HOUSE GOES BLACK

Death had a profound impact on the politics and culture of the United States. On 20 February 1862, William 'Willie' Wallace Lincoln, the third son of President Abraham Lincoln and First Lady, Mary Todd Lincoln, died at the age of 12. His loss profoundly affected the Lincoln family and cast a shadow over the White House during a critical period in American history, the ongoing Civil War (1861–5).

Willie's illness began in early 1862 at the White House. Both Willie and his younger brother, Tad, fell ill with what was diagnosed as typhoid fever, again likely due to contaminated water at the White House.

Despite the best medical care available, Willie's condition steadily deteriorated. The fever persisted, accompanied by severe weakness and dehydration. His parents were deeply distressed, with both Abraham and Mary spending long hours at his bedside, hoping for his recovery. However, the lack of adequate treatments for his fever meant their hopes were in vain.

Willie Lincoln succumbed to illness on 20 February 1862, devastating his parents. Abraham Lincoln, known for his stoicism, shortly after being delivered the fateful news, burst into his secretary's office, John Nicolay, sobbing, 'My boy is gone. He is actually gone!', a rare emotional outburst that underscored the depth of his grief. Although Lincoln continued to perform his presidential duties, those close to him noted a significant change in his demeanour, marked by increased melancholy and introspection.

Mary Todd Lincoln was even more profoundly affected by the loss of her son. Already prone to emotional instability, she plunged into a deep depression from which she never fully recovered. Her grief was compounded by guilt, as Mary blamed herself for not doing more to protect her son. Mary's mourning took on an obsessive nature: she often visited Willie's grave and kept his room in the White House exactly as it had been when he was alive.

The impact of Willie's death on the White House was significant. The residence, which had already been a place of anxiety due to the ongoing war, was sent down a path of

William 'Willie' Wallace Lincoln two years before he died of typhoid fever.

mourning and depression over the Lincolns' personal tragedy, and staff and visitors alike noted the oppressive air of sorrow that hung over the household.

Willie's death also influenced Abraham Lincoln's perspective on life and leadership. His personal loss deepened his empathy and resolve as he continued to guide the burgeoning nation through its darkest period. The Lincolns' grief became emblematic of the broader suffering endured from the some 600,000 deaths and widespread devastation suffered across the country. The brutality of battle, combined with the horror of disease, starvation and the impact left on war-shattered families left deep scars on the American psyche that would endure for generations, some, arguably felt to this day.

The relentless grip of disease did not discriminate, claiming the lives of American presidents and their children within the very walls of the White House. Across the Atlantic, European royalty fared no better, as the opulent courts of kings and queens became equally haunted by the spectre of death.

ROYALTY AND DEATH

The Russian Imperial family faced multiple tragedies due to haemophilia, a genetic disorder that also affected many male descendants of Queen Victoria, including her son and four grandsons.

Alexei Nikolaevich, the last tsesarevich of Russia, was born on 12 August 1904. He was the only son of Tsar Nicholas II and heir to the Romanov throne, and was born with haemophilia, inherited from Empress Alexandra Feodorovna, his mother and the granddaughter of Queen Victoria. His family, desperate for a cure, employed the 'powers' of the mystic Rasputin, who claimed to alleviate the boy's suffering. He did not.

In 1917, Nicholas II abdicated in favour of his brother, Grand Duke Michael, who refused the crown the following day, leaving Russia without a legitimate monarchy. The power vacuum intensified political chaos, fueling revolutionary fervour. Without a clear leader, the Provisional Government was unable to stabilize the nation, ultimately leading to Bolshevik control. But it was not haemophilia that killed Alexei. After months held in captivity by Bolshevik revolutionaries, the 13-year old, along with other members of his family, was executed on 17 July 1918, in Yekaterinburg, Russia, marking the tragic end of the Romanov dynasty.

Disease is classless, impacting the wealthy as well as the poor, and history is filled with examples of this. Typhoid fever is caused by the bacterium *Salmonella typhi*, typically transmitted through contaminated food or water. In Victorian Britain, sanitary conditions, even in royal households, were not rigorously upheld, making the spread of such disease common. Prince Albert, the Queen's consort, is believed to have contracted typhoid through contaminated drinking water at Windsor Castle, where the sanitation infrastructure was inadequate.

The illness began to manifest in the prince during early December 1861. His symptoms

Prince Albert Victor's funeral service at St George's Chapel, Windsor Castle.

included high fever, abdominal pain and severe diarrhoea. Despite the best efforts of the royal physicians, his condition worsened. Medical knowledge and treatments for typhoid fever in the mid-nineteenth century were limited, and the standard care did little more than alleviate symptoms. The prince's fever persisted, leading to a weakened state and severe dehydration, his health rapidly declining over two weeks. As the infection progressed, it likely led to septicemia, a life-threatening condition where the infection spreads into the bloodstream, causing widespread inflammation and organ failure.

On 14 December 1861, Prince Albert succumbed to the illness, surrounded by his family. The official cause of death was recorded as typhoid fever, although some modern historians suggest that he may have suffered from Crohn's disease, based on reports that Prince Albert complained of ongoing stomach pain and gastro complications that were not fully understood at the time, which predisposed him to what were to be fatal complications.

The prince's death deeply affected Queen Victoria, plunging her into a prolonged period of mourning that defined the rest of her reign, and spread a pall of melancholy across Britain, the continent and the United States for decades, impacting on culture, society and healthcare. Prince Albert's death underscored the need for improved public health measures and sanitation, a realization that gradually led to significant health reforms in Britain.

On mainland Europe, the death of Princess Maria Annunciata similarly brought home that no one was safe from the perils of deadly disease. In 1862, aged 19, Maria Annunciata married Archduke Karl Ludwig of Austria, the younger

Queen Victoria's five daughters, Alice, Helena,
Beatrice, Victoria and Louise, in mourning, 1862.

brother of Emperor Franz Joseph I of Austria. This union solidified ties between two powerful European royal houses, the House of Bourbon and the House of Habsburg, and further positioned Maria Annunciata as a figure of dynastic importance.

Throughout her life, Maria Annunciata struggled with what was likely tuberculosis, historical records citing her symptoms as chronic coughing, fatigue, weight loss and fever – consistent with the disease. Like many members of European royalty at the time, she was frequently subjected to contemporary medical treatments, including blood-letting, purging and the use of herbal remedies. These practices did little to address the underlying cause of her health problems, however.

The prince's death deeply affected Queen Victoria, plunging her into a prolonged period of mourning.

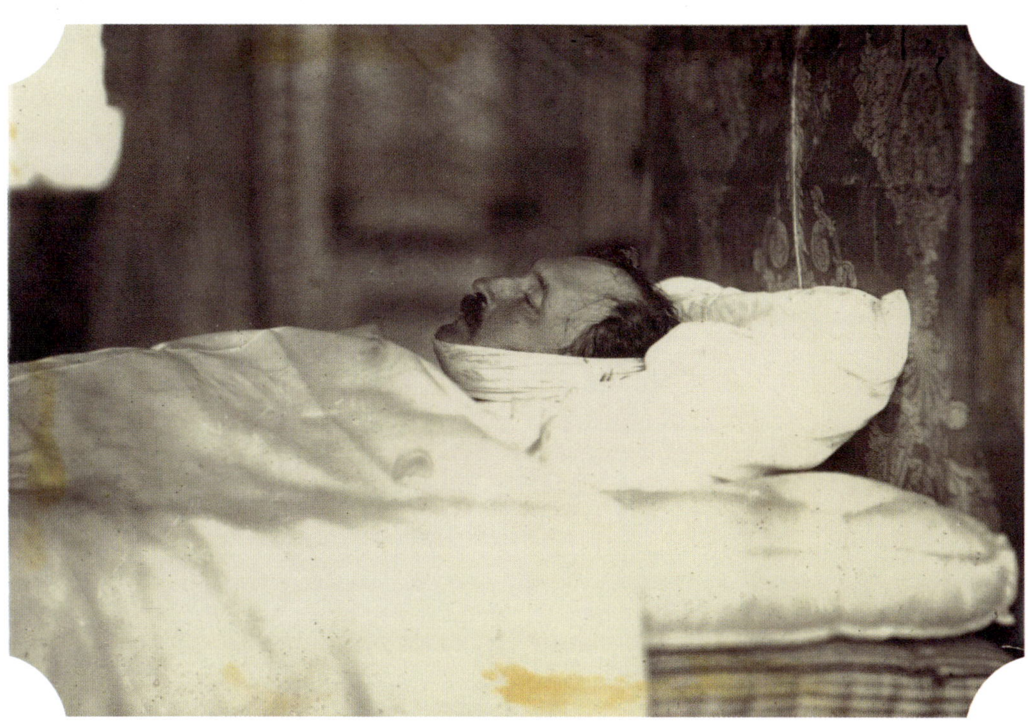

A deceased Prince Albert in the Blue Room of Windsor Castle.

A watercolour of Princess Maria Annunciata of Bourbon-Two Sicilies on her deathbed.

By 1871, Maria Annunciata's condition had worsened to such a degree that she spent her final months in seclusion, reports indicating that she had become increasingly frail and was bedridden. On 4 May of that year, she died, aged just 28, leaving behind a grieving family, and a young son, Franz Ferdinand, whose death several decades later would have such a devastating effect on the world. The assassination of Archduke Franz Ferdinand, heir to the Austro-Hungarian throne, on 28 June 1914, in Sarajevo, by Serbian nationalist Gavrilo Princip, was the spark that led to the First World War. Austria–Hungary, with Germany's support, issued an ultimatum (to publicly condemn the "dangerous propaganda" against Austria-Hungary) to Serbia, blaming it for the assassination. Serbia, backed by Russia, refused to fully comply. Franz Ferdinand's death set light to a powder keg of nationalism and militarism, forging alliances – Russia mobilizing to defend Serbia, Germany declaring war on Russia and France and Britain soon entering the conflict – that would lead to a four-year global conflict, the impact of which still resonates. ❀

CHAPTER II

In the SHADOW *of the* SCYTHE

LIFE AND DEATH IN THE VICTORIAN ERA

SICKNESS, INFANT MORTALITY AND THE AVERAGE LIFESPAN

'E*nter the hospital as a patient, leave as a corpse.*' This grim saying was often murmured over warm ales in dimly lit taverns by those fretting over the fate of relatives in hospitals in the Western world of the late 1800s.

From the mid-1800s to the early 1900s, hospitals were mired in the medical limitations and inadequate sanitary practices of the time. The wards were often overcrowded and under-resourced, echoing with the groans of the afflicted, who lay in tightly packed rows of rudimentary beds. The air was heavy with the stench of illness and, if lucky, the sharp tang of carbolic acid, used in a desperate attempt to disinfect and ward off the ever-looming threat of cross-infection.

Upon admission, a patient would be struck by the bleak surroundings – a bitter reminder that the hope of recovery was probably not to be found here. If they were one of many stricken with typhoid, they would have been suffering high fever, severe headache and intense stomach pain – which would soon escalate. As the disease progressed, the sufferer's abdomen would swell and an intense rash of rose-coloured spots would appear on their chest and stomach. Delirium set in, with patients murmuring incoherently or crying out in fevered hallucinations.

Medical treatment was rudimentary and largely ineffective against the typhoid pathogen *Salmonella typhi bacteria*. Doctors, draped in black coats, their faces often grim with the knowledge of their patients' likely fates, administered concoctions of various herbs and opiates that did little more than offer temporary relief from pain. No antibiotic treatment was available; such a medical breakthrough was decades away. Instead, treatments focused on managing symptoms, and included interventions like cold compresses to reduce fever, or mercury compounds that promised a cure but often, in fact, contributed to the patient's additional suffering.

Nurses, clad in long, starched uniforms, moved from bed to bed, changing soiled linens and offering sips of water or weak broth to parched lips. Their faces offered brief solace, though they, too, were often overwhelmed by the sheer number of patients and the dire nature of their wards.

As days turned into weeks, bodies weakened under the relentless assault of the multiplying bacteria. Intestinal haemorrhaging was a common complication, leading to further debilitation. The patient's immediate world, filled with other sufferers, provided constant reminders of their likely grim outcome, as fellow patients died. In the final stages, the person's struggle would become palpably more desperate. Family members, if allowed visitation, would gather around the bed, their faces creased with worry and sorrow, whispering words of love even as they braced themselves for the inevitable.

The patient would slip in and out of consciousness, each breath more laboured than

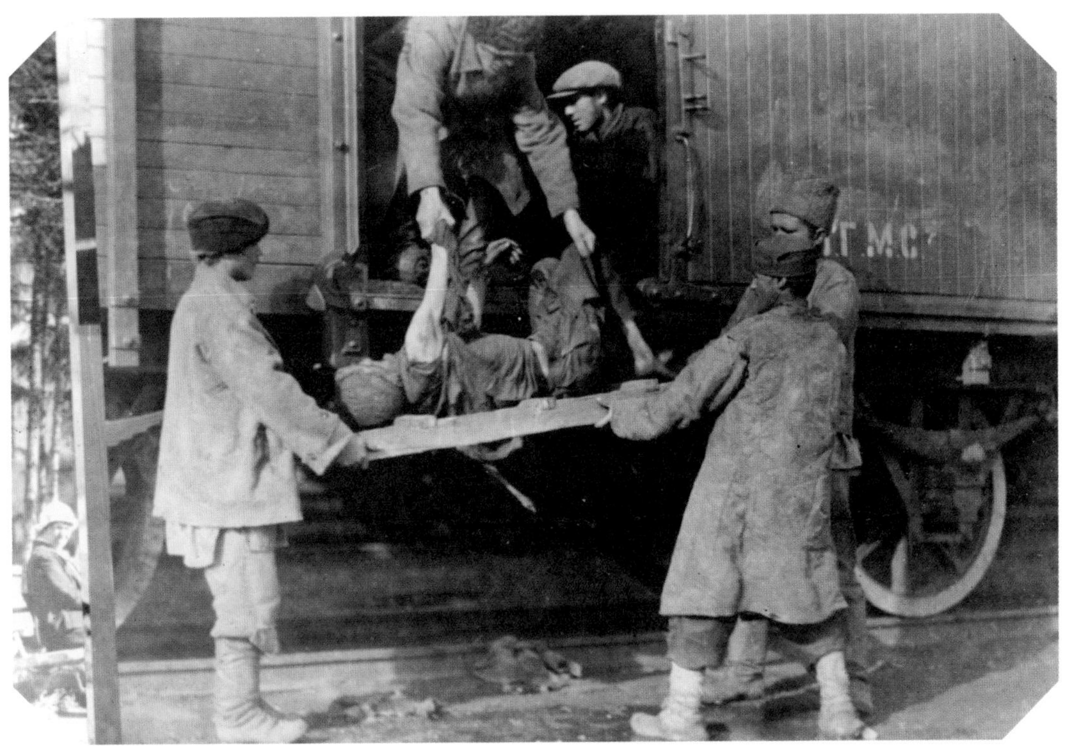

A dramatic image of a volunteer loading a corpse. A person who lost their battle with typhus fever.

the last, their eyes sunken, as fever scorched their fragile frame. Chilled sweats and delirium blurred the world around them. In the flickering gas lamplights, cries of the dying echoed, but no comfort came. Breath faltered, and death slipped in quietly – leaving behind only silence and the scent of decay. In the hushed aftermath, nurses would gently prepare the deceased for their final journey, and the ward would absorb yet another loss, a solemn reminder of the cruel reach of typhoid fever which served as a stark example of the broader societal issues of the time.

In the Victorian era, tuberculosis (TB), or consumption as it was commonly known, was a major cause of mortality in both the latter and the United Kingdom. In the United States, at the turn of the twentieth century, it was estimated that 450 people died each day from tuberculosis, most, between the ages of 15 and 44.[2] This high death toll reflects the disease's widespread impact during this period.

In the United Kingdom, between 1851 and 1910, approximately four million people died from consumption. The disease accounted for nearly 25 per cent of all deaths during the 1850s.[3] This high mortality rate can be attributed to the living conditions, as increasing numbers moved from agricultural to urban areas for work, living in overpopulated areas, with poor sanitation and contaminated water supplies, which facilitated the spread of diseases like TB. These figures underscore the devastating impact of tuberculosis in the Victorian era, highlighting it as one of the major public health challenges of the time.

DEATH BY WATER

During the late 1800s and early 1900s, in both England and the United States, one of the most critical infrastructure failures was the sheer inadequacy of sewer and waste disposal systems, which severely impacted on public health. Human waste and industrial pollutants often ended up in the same waterways that supplied drinking water, and directly contributed to the spread of disease, significantly impacting infant mortality rates.

In England, in 1858, the situation was epitomized by London's infamous 'Great Stink', where the smell of untreated human waste emanating from the River Thames became unbearable, catalyzing the government to undertake significant improvements in sewage management. Despite such efforts, many areas of the city remained poorly served well into the twentieth century, fostering conditions ripe for disease.

The common illnesses resulting from these inadequate sewer systems were primarily waterborne-related. Cholera, an often fatal disease, flourished in environments where water supplies were contaminated with sewage. It surpassed other diseases in its deadly toll. Originating from contaminated food or water, cholera's impact was devastating and immediate, with victims suffering from severe dehydration due to relentless vomiting and diarrhea. The disease acted quickly, and in densely populated urban areas, it spread like wildfire, leaving communities in mourning and crippling entire neighbourhoods.

Cholera wasn't the only disease to fear, however. Infectious waterborne and airborne diseases thrived in the crowded living conditions of urban areas, affecting the organs and gradually breaking down their victims' bodies. The impact of the unsanitary conditions in which most people lived on infant mortality was particularly disturbing. Outbreaks of dysentery, an infection of the intestines causing severe diarrhea, with blood and mucus, were prevalent in areas with poor sanitation, where access to clean water was limited, and where multiple families might share a single toilet, if any were, indeed, available.

Infants and young children are more vulnerable to the effects of diarrheal diseases due to their less developed immune systems and smaller body mass. Historical records indicate that in England and the United States, high infant

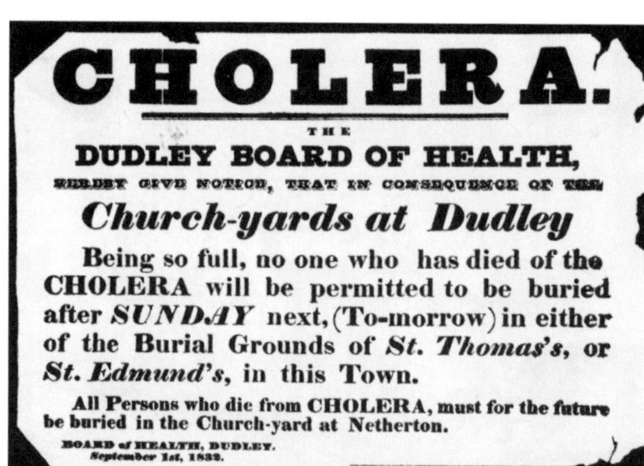

CHOLERA.

THE

DUDLEY BOARD OF HEALTH,

HEREBY GIVE NOTICE, THAT IN CONSEQUENCE OF THE

Church-yards at Dudley

Being so full, no one who has died of the CHOLERA will be permitted to be buried after *SUNDAY* next, (To-morrow) in either of the Burial Grounds of *St. Thomas's*, or *St. Edmund's*, in this Town.

All Persons who die from CHOLERA, must for the future be buried in the Church-yard at Netherton.

BOARD of HEALTH, DUDLEY.
September 1st, 1832.

W. MAURICE, PRINTER, HIGH STREET, DUDLEY

A notice that the burial grounds at the Church Yards at Dudley are full due to the cholera epidemic.

mortality rates were closely correlated with such insanitary conditions. For example, during cholera outbreaks, the mortality rate among infants and young children was disproportionally high compared to other age groups.

Before the age of five, 35 out of every 45 children[4] had experienced measles, smallpox, scarlet fever, diphtheria and other diseases. In the United States, the statistics were just as dismal, with up to 34 per cent of children dying before their fifth birthday.[5]

During this period, there was a litany of fatal maladies that resulted in horrific suffering, countless deaths and heartbreak for their surviving family members.

THE TERRIBLE THREE

Among the many competing diseases of the time, a few stood out. Smallpox, also known as 'the speckled monster', was feared by all. Caused by the variola virus, it was ruthless, extremely contagious and during certain periods of the 1800s claimed the lives of more than 30 per cent of those infected.[6] Symptoms begin with fever, fatigue and severe headaches, followed by a distinctive, painful rash and pustules. The virus often leads to organ failure, respiratory complications and sepsis, which can ultimately result in death. Again, children, with their undeveloped immune systems, were especially vulnerable. Those who survived the disease were often left blind, disabled or with severe facial scarring, their lives forever altered.

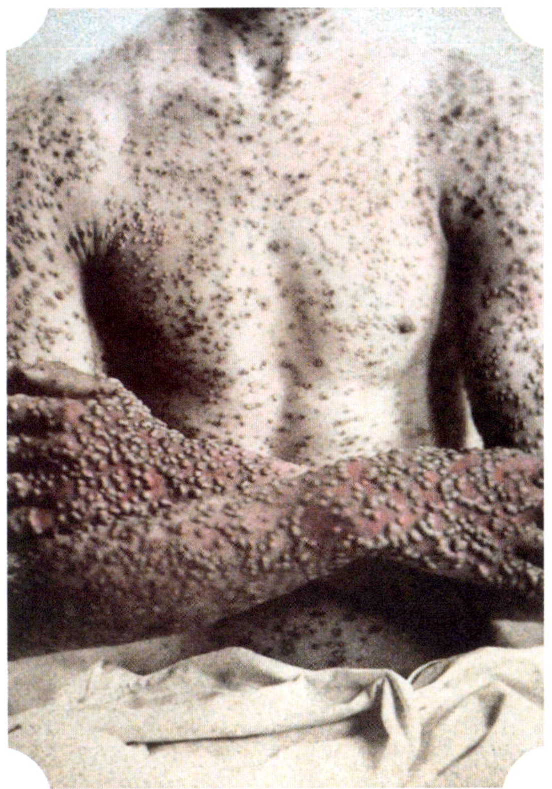

A medical photo, c.1886, documenting a severe case of variola, a strain of smallpox.

Scarlet fever, a bacterial infection caused by *Streptococcus pyogenes*, transmitted through respiratory droplets or contact with infected surfaces, also cast a shadow over the nineteenth century, particularly affecting the young. Symptoms include high fever, sore throat and a red, sandpaper-like rash, and with the absence of antibiotics at the time the infection often lead to severe complications like rheumatic fever, sepsis,

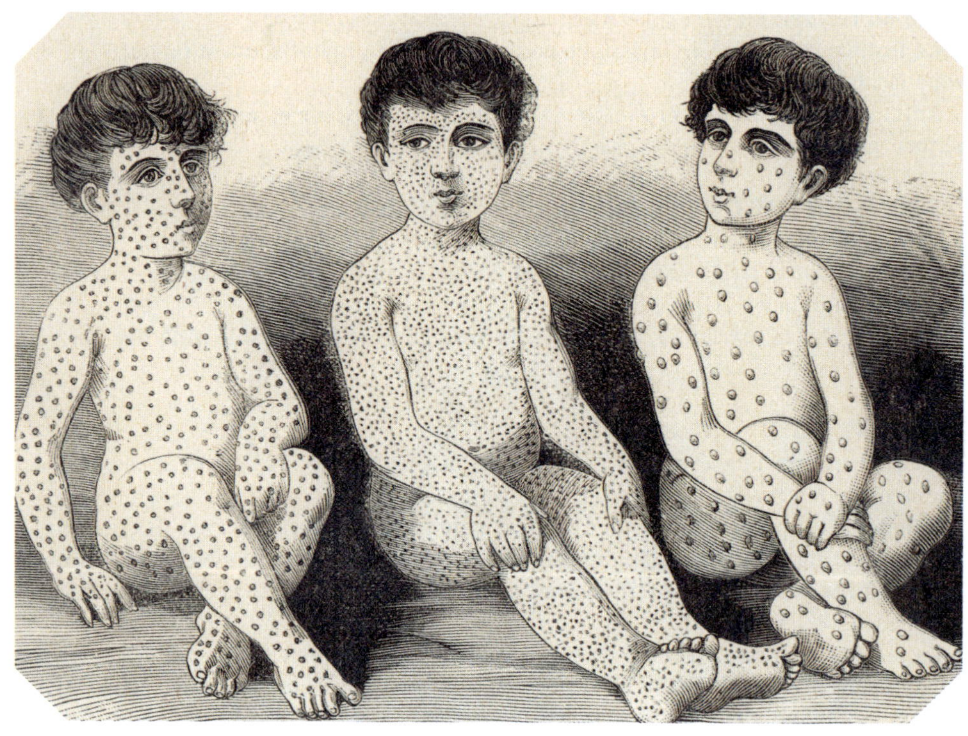

An illustration from a medical journal c.1880 depicting children stricken with measles, scarlet fever, and smallpox.

and organ damage, potentially resulting in death.

As industrialization continued to surge and urban populations swelled, poor living conditions and overcrowding became common in burgeoning cities on both sides of the Atlantic. In these cramped environments, scarlet fever spread with alarming ease, its bacterial tendrils thriving in the filth and close quarters, often proving fatal for the children it infected.

In the United States, outbreaks of malaria were a recurring nightmare, beginning as far back as 1830. It particularly decimated indigeous populations who were already struggling with displacement, loss of traditional lands and lifestyles, poverty and malnutrition. The annual bouts of malaria, transmitted by mosquitoes thriving in the American landscape, particularly in swampy areas, were relentless. Select historical accounts including that of Robert Boyd, anthropologist, author, and affiliated research professor in the Anthropology Department at Portland State University suggests that malaria may have been as deadly, as the first smallpox epidemics of the 1600s and 1700s. Introduced by European settlers some estimate up to 90 per cent of certain indigenous communities groups were wiped out, most notably the Powhatan Confederacy of Virginia, the Wampanoag of New England, the Choctaw, Chickasaw, and Creek of the North American Southeast and the Timucua of Florida. The death tolls among these tribes are estimated to range anywhere from 300,000 to 500,000.

MALADIES, MIASMA AND BLACK MAGIC

During the Victorian era, the medical field was still developing. The germ theory of disease, which posits that micro-organisms are the cause of many diseases, was not widely accepted until the late nineteenth century. Prior to this, miasma theory dominated, that is that diseases were 'miasmas', inhaling 'bad air', infected by rotting matter, such as decomposing bodies and vegetation. This fundamental misunderstanding of disease causation underpinned many of the limitations in medical science during not just the nineteenth century but well into the twentieth century, too.

During the 1854 London cholera outbreak, estimated to have claimed more than 600 lives, physician Dr John Snow challenged miasma theory. He had published a paper in the later 1840s suggesting that cholera was waterborne, which contradicted the prevailing bad air theory and was initially met with scepticism. However, following the 1854 outbreak, Snow traced the source to a contaminated water pump in Broad Street, in Soho, by tracking the locations of cholera-related deaths. A leaking sewer impacted the well from which the water was drawn. This was a pivotal moment in public healthcare, although it took several years for Snow's theories to be taken seriously – really only after the 1866 cholera epidemic did it lead to the implementation of more sanitary water and waste systems.

The ignorance towards germs and their role in disease transmission, however, extended to the medical community, where doctors and nurses often did not wash their hands or sterilize their instruments between patients. One of the most striking examples is from the work of Dr Ignaz Semmelweis, a Hungarian physician and scientist who, in 1847, observed that women giving birth in hospitals had a higher mortality rate from puerperal fever (postpartum infection of a woman's reproductive tract) than those giving birth at home. He attributed this to medical staff going directly from autopsies to delivering babies without washing their hands, thus carrying diseased cadaverous material from the autopsy room into birthing areas of the hospital.

Despite his efforts to institute hand-washing practices via research papers and authoring books on the topic, Semmelweis' views on cross-contamination, although supported by most physicians in the UK, were highly criticized by the medical community in the rest of Europe, leading to his professional isolation. This rejection, combined with signs of his own cognitive decline – likely from Alzheimer's or advanced syphilis, a disease many obstetricians unknowingly contracted after years of examining patients – made Semmelweis vulnerable. His erratic behavior was used as an excuse to place him in a mental institution, where he was held against his will, brutally beaten and where he ultimately died under suspicious circumstances only two weeks after being institutionalized – a tragic end to his life and legacy.

In the United States, similar problems and unhelpful practices prevailed. The American Civil War exposed the inadequacies in medical knowledge and practice – more soldiers died from disease than from wounds sustained in battle. The lack of effective antiseptic techniques and the rudimentary nature of surgical practices led to high mortality rates from infection.

Surgeries at this time were often performed without any attempt to maintain a sterile environment, especially on the battlefield. Surgeons typically wore their everyday clothes and operated in rooms that were not sanitized, leading to high rates of post-surgical infection. A notorious example is the popularity of operating theatres, where surgeries were performed in front of medical students in amphitheatre-like rooms that were rarely cleaned. This lack of sterilization, combined with the use of unsterilized surgical instruments, contributed to a high death rate following surgeries.

In normal hospitals, overcrowding, inadequate ventilation and insufficient sanitation were common issues, therefore making them breeding grounds for infection. Thus, a hospital stay for something as non-life-threatening as a broken arm could easily prove fatal.

The design of many hospitals did not allow for thorough cleaning, in the way we would expect in the twenty-first century. Developments and innovations in building materials and cleaning products have brought us to a different place, in the Western world, certainly. But in the nineteenth century, porous wooden floors and walls harboured pathogens from blood or bodily fluids that dripped or splattered from diseased patients suffering all manner of ailments. Floors were often covered in sawdust to absorb blood during surgeries which was then swept away, possibly days later, without any disinfection of the surface below.

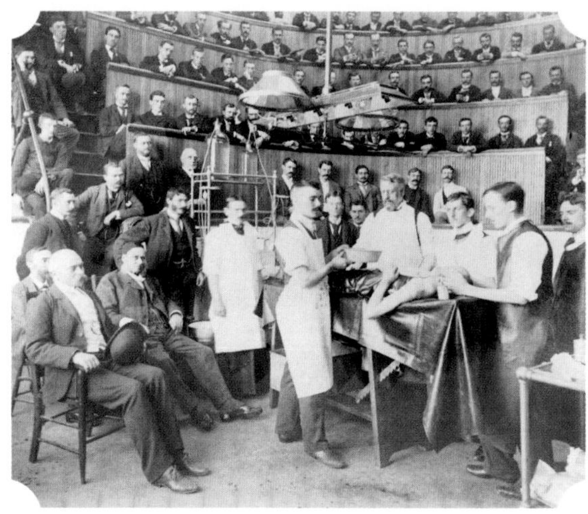

An early surgical procedure at Bellevue Medical Center in New York City.

For many, living in close proximity to a local hospital arguably might be a comforting factor regarding medical care, however it brought issues with it in Victorian times. Proper disposal of medical waste was virtually non-existent. It would be decades before the removal of bio-hazardous material would be relegated to 'safe' disposal areas. This highly infectious refuse of blood-soaked saw dust, used bandages, soiled linens and other materials contaminated with bodily fluids was either left to rot behind the medical facility or found its way into the Thames or the local dump, and many times into the local drinking water.

This problem was only exacerbated in urban areas with a high population density surrounding the medical facilities and the poor sanitation infrastructure.

The mid-nineteenth century saw a dramatic increase in the number of new doctors in the United States. In 1810, less than 400 people received medical degrees, however by 1859, that number grew exponentially to 17,213.[7]

However, in the early to mid-1800s, the path to becoming a physician differed from the rigorous medical education and licensing processes we

A formal portrait of Florence Nightingale was taken somewhere between 1860-1870.

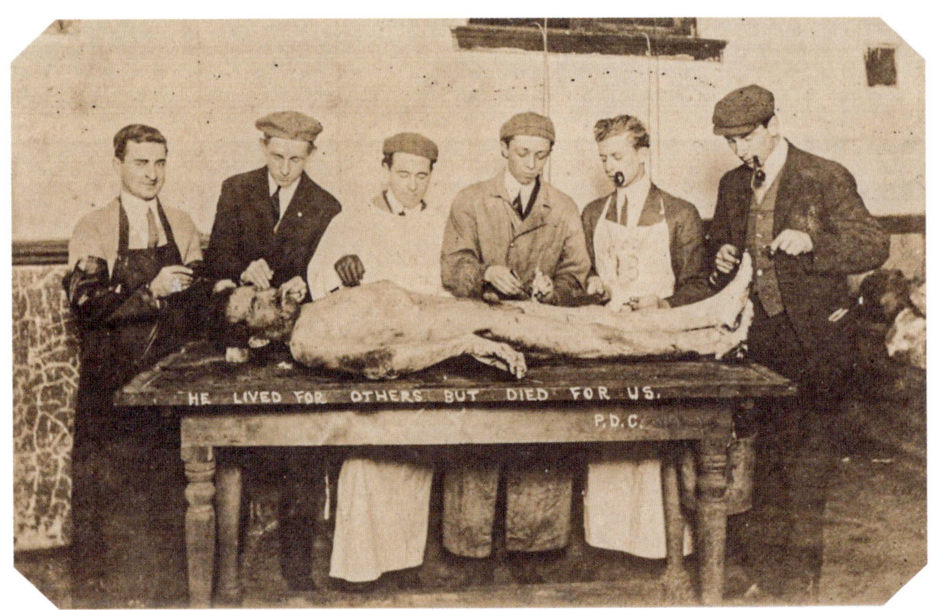

For medical students of the era it was common to have photos taken with their cadaver. Here, six medical students pose behind their cadaver in a staged photo.

see today. In both the United Kingdom and the United States, the journey to medical practice often lacked formalized standards and varied significantly depending on one's geographical location, educational institution and social connections. There existed a stark division among doctors: those who acquired their medical knowledge solely through apprenticeships, devoid of any formal medical school training, those who possessed formal medical school degrees, often after completing apprenticeships and those who merely paid a "tuition fee" to an unscrupulous medical school official in exchange for a license. This contrast in educational backgrounds led to significant disparities in medical expertise.

Regrettably, the mid-1800s saw a dearth of formal education in medical schools. The admission requirements were lenient, with no undergraduate degree necessary. Even the most esteemed institutions, like Harvard Medical School, resembled trade schools more than centres of academic excellence.

In the 1850s, the Harvard faculty comprised practicing physicians from the nearby Massachusetts General Hospital who designed the curriculum and established the requirements to graduate. In the first year, students would have to complete two sixteen-week lecture courses, and in the following year, they would have to attend those exact same lectures. This method of teaching was common practice in the United States, based on the belief that repetition was the key to learning medicine. Upon completion of this two-year programme, students were required to write a medical thesis and pass an oral exam.

Regardless of how these men and women acquired their medical education, it is safe to say it was marked by significant deficiencies in the importance of medical hygiene, largely due to a lack of understanding of disease transmission and, at times, inadequate medical education. In addition, there was still a prevalent belief among some segments of society that supernatural forces, including black magic or witchcraft, could cause illness or misfortune. This belief was particularly persistent in rural or less scientifically educated communities in the United Kingdom and the United States.

A complex intersection of emerging scientific understandings and long-standing superstitions marked the period. While the more educated and urban populations were increasingly influenced by scientific advances, including the beginnings of what we understand as modern medical science, many rural communities held onto traditional beliefs, including those involving the paranormal.

Attempts to educate the masses were reflected in legislation. In Britain, the Witchcraft Act of 1735 shifted the legal perspective from punishing the practice of witchcraft to punishing the claim of magical powers, with the aim of discouraging belief in such phenomena by treating it as fraudulent rather than genuine threat. However, it wasn't entirely effective at eradicating these beliefs, and they continued to influence how some people interpreted the causes of disease.

HUMORALISM AND THE VICTORIAN LOVE OF TOXIC SUBSTANCES

If you were lucky or wealthy enough to find your way into a 'legitimate' physician's office you might have regretted your good fortune based on the type of treatment administered in an attempt to cure your ills.

One of the more common catch-all remedies was bloodletting, which involved withdrawing often significant quantities of blood from a patient to cure or prevent illness and disease. Rooted in ancient medical theories of humoralism, which theorized that balance among the body's four humorus – blood, phlegm, black bile and yellow bile – was essential for health, bloodletting was used to treat a vast range of ailments from headaches to heart disease. Physicians employed lancets to cut into a patient's veins, and were also widely used, especially for more precise or controlled bloodletting. It persisted into the Victorian-era despite increasing evidence of its ineffectiveness and risk to patients. In the early twentieth century, some doctors even recommended it in the treatment of pneumonia, but today bloodletting is a largely disused practice.

In the pre-antibiotic world, mercury was a commonly used panacea, particularly for treating syphilis – a rampant and, for many, fatal disease. Known as 'blue mass', mercury treatments could involve taking pills containing the element, applying mercury ointments to lesions or even injecting mercury directly into the body. The toxic effects of mercury were not well understood in the nineteenth century, and patients often suffered from associated poisoning, exhibiting such symptoms as tooth loss, neurological and severe digestive system damage.

The alternative to mercury was equally as

A lithographic plate showing women outside a pharmacy selling leeches and tooth powder (c.1845).

dangerous, however. Arsenic, a known poison, was paradoxically used as a treatment for a variety of ailments, including the previously mentioned syphilis, skin diseases and as a component of many over-the-counter tonics and health pills. Victorian doctors prescribed it for everything from asthma to cancer, unaware of its cumulative toxic effects.

Arsenic was such a ubiquitous substance that it was used from everything from women's make-up to murder weapons. During the 1800s, the pursuit of beauty led some women to use arsenic as a cosmetic, despite the rumours of its toxicity. It was prized for its reputed ability to impart a pale, translucent skin tone, highly coveted as a symbol of beauty and social status. Marketed in various forms, including arsenic wafers and complexion powders, it was used to achieve the desirable 'arsenic complexion'. The use of arsenic-based products was a dangerous practice, as prolonged exposure could lead to severe health consequences, including organ damage and death.

In the late 1800s, cocaine was initially hailed as a miracle drug and was widely prescribed for a variety of ailments, including pain relief, depression and as a cure for morphine addiction. Marketed as a non-addictive substance, it was included in numerous medical products, such as tonics and even popular beverages like the original formula of Coca-Cola. This widespread medical endorsement contributed to its popularity before its addictive properties and harmful effects were fully understood.

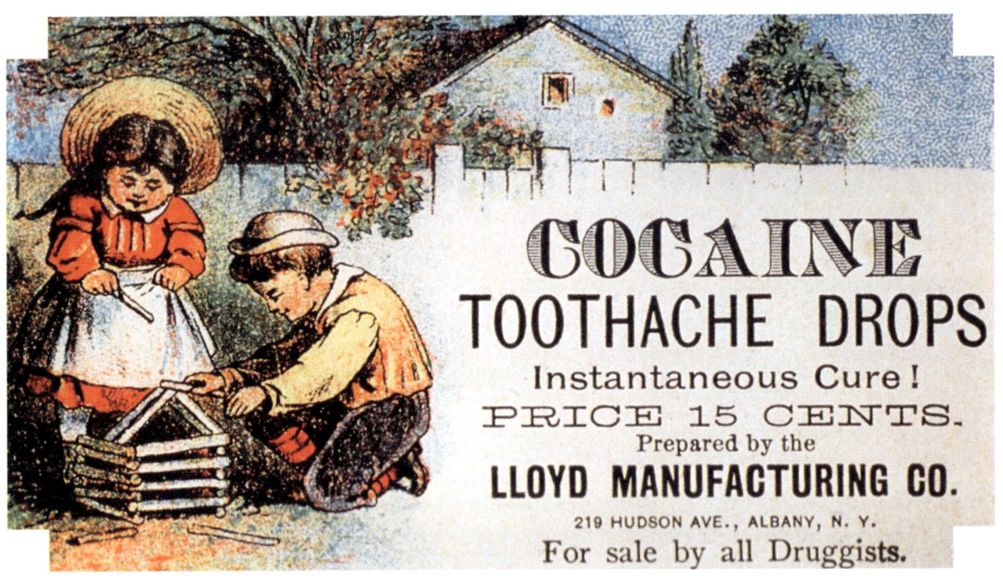

Today, we find it odd that cocaine would be an over-the-counter remedy. When suggested it be administered to children, it was shocking.

ELECTRICITY AND MEDICAL AILMENTS

During this same era, the public fascination with electricity led to the emergence of numerous electrical devices marketed with exaggerated claims of health benefits. These quack devices, often sold with sensational advertising, purported to cure ailments ranging from headaches to rheumatism using electrical currents. Such gadgets reflected both the excitement and the limited understanding of electricity's medical potential at the time, with many devices having no proven effectiveness, and some being outright dangerous.

One of the more popular electrotherapy devices was the Davis & Kidder's Patent Magneto-Electric Machine for Nervous Diseases. The inventor Ari Davis was granted a patent for his invention in 1854. Davis was not a doctor nor a scientist; however, he sold the patent for his device in that same year to Dr Walter Kidder. A year later, Kidder sold the rights to his brother-in-law, William Henry Burnap, a marketing genius. He introduced it to the curious masses with great success.

The machine claimed to cure, or at least *relieve*, symptoms of everything from toothaches to gangrene and listlessness, via a series of low- and high-voltage bolts of electricity administered to the skin/nerves through rods and paddles attached to a portable handcranked electrical generator. Extensive directions and 'tips and tricks' on how to best use the machine were plastered on the inside lid of the device.

Did it actually work? The short answer is no; at least not in the way it was advertised. The machine might have had some perceived benefits, but they were likely due to the placebo effect. Patients could experience temporary relief simply because they believed in the treatment or the electrical stimulation distracted them from their symptoms.

There is a grain of truth to the idea that electrical stimulation can relieve temporary pain or muscle relaxation. This principle is similar to modern TENS (Transcutaneous Electrical Nerve Stimulation) units used to alleviate pain. However, the technology and understanding of how electrical impulses affect the body were primitive then, and any positive effects would have been inconsistent.

Victorian society was fascinated by electricity, which was cutting-edge, and the machine fitted neatly into the era's obsession with technology and the belief that electricity could restore vitality and cure diseases. However, it was also part of a broader trend of quack medical devices that promised miraculous cures but often delivered little more than perceived temporary relief from any symptoms.

An equally bizarre use of electricity, but with significant contributions to medical science, was the work of Guillaume-Benjamin Duchenne, a French neurologist who, in the mid-1800s, revolutionized the understanding of muscle physiology through his work with électropuncture (electrotherapy).

Duchenne used electric currents to stimulate muscles and nerves, a method that allowed him to chart and explore the muscular system in unprecedented detail. He induced muscle contractions by applying electrodes to specific points on the skin, demonstrating how electrical stimulation could control and influence muscular movements.

Duchenne believed the human face was a map, its features codifiable into a universal system of classification of mental states/emotions, and that facial expressions were a gateway to the soul. His experiments and photography culminated in the 1862 publication, *The Mechanism of Human Physiognomy*, (also titled *The Electro-Physiological Analysis of the Expression of the Passions, Applicable to the Practice of the Plastic Arts*). His findings formed the basis for our understanding of neuromuscular disorders, including the eponymous Duchenne muscular dystrophy.

MENTAL HEALTH AND MISDIAGNOSIS – PHRENOLOGY, HYSTERIA

Phrenology was not as physically dangerous but possibly a bit more sinister. It was a pseudoscience that involved measuring bumps on the skull to predict mental traits and was taken quite seriously by many in the medical community. Phrenologists claimed that they could diagnose not only mental traits but also moral character and predispositions to certain types of illnesses based on the shape and size of various parts of the skull. This practice influenced not only medical treatments but also societal decisions such as marriages, business partnerships and criminal sentencing.

Being misdiagnosed was also a common issue during this era, mainly due to the limited medical knowledge and diagnostic tools available at the time. Diseases were often diagnosed based on symptoms rather than underlying causes, leading to treatments that were ineffective or even harmful.

An early 20th-century photo of a woman under hypnosis gripped in hysteria.

A notable example of misdiagnosis was the treatment of 'hysteria', which was commonly diagnosed in women and today is discredited as a condition. The symptoms of hysteria were vague and varied, including fainting, nervousness and insomnia, which today might be recognized as symptoms of psychological disorders, anaemia, epilepsy or something completely different. Treatments for hysteria included confinement, the administration of sedatives and other more invasive procedures, which often did not address the actual health needs of the patients, such as the use of vibrators, a practice that emerged from the medical community's efforts to embrace the attitude of better living through psychological applications and technological advancements and offer remedies through therapeutic interventions and mechanical inventions. This practice was rooted in the belief that hysteria was related to women's sexuality and reproductive organs, and physicians employed vibrators as a clinical tool to induce 'hysterical paroxysm', which we now recognize as orgasm. The use of vibrators was considered a legitimate and efficient way to manage and treat hysteria, reflecting the period's medical misunderstanding of women's health.

The Victorian era hospitals were far from being sanctuaries and often the scene of suffering and death. Deadly illnesses ravaged the population, especially in overcrowded urban centres and widespread suffering underscored the urgent need for advancements in public health.

For most Victorians, being ill during this era more often than not ended up with the patient suffering a lifelong, chronic, incurable condition, disfigured or in a pine box. Plus, many of the 'medicines' prescribed rarely treated the conditions for which they were purchased, and often contained harmful substances like alcohol, opium, arsenic or mercury, or as we have seen, cocaine, leading to addiction and other health issues.

However, despite the dark conditions, the period was also a time of significant transition. With medical pioneers beginning to challenge prevailing beliefs about disease transmission, pushing the boundaries of understanding with groundbreaking work on sanitation and hygiene, despite the reluctance to accept these medical facts and persist with the miasma theory and entrenched superstitions.

Looking forward, there was hope that improved sanitation, coupled with scientific advancements, could transform public health. The implementation of sewer systems and a gradual acceptance of antiseptic practices laid the groundwork for modern medicine. As the century turned, the foundations were set for discoveries that would usher in an era of antibiotics and vaccines, offering hope for a future where the grim spectre of epidemic diseases could possibly be conquered. ❀

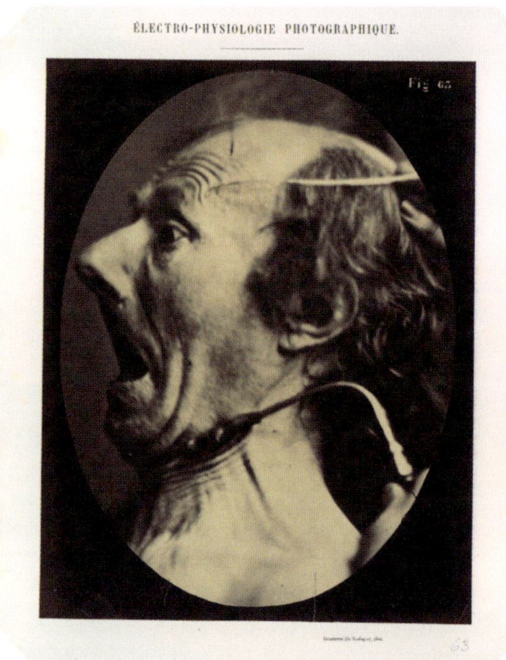

Guillaume-Benjamin-Amand Duchenne de Boulogne, a French neurologistr, generates 'the Expression of terror' on a subject using electrodes.

A 19th-century drawing showing a physician massaging the genitalia of a female patient suffering from hysteria.

CHAPTER III

MOURNING COUTURE

DYING'S INFLUENCE OVER FASHION

THE WIDOW'S WEEDS

In the Victorian period, mourning was not merely a private affair but a public performance, replete with detailed rules on attire, duration and behaviour, especially for the wealthy and the nobility. For these social classes, mourning attire was as much a statement of status and fashion as it was a symbol of grief. This dual adherence to mourning customs and fashion norms demonstrated the societal layers and complexities when dealing with death and remembrance in this period.

In the aftermath of a loved one's passing on, women navigated the complex terrain of grief through a structured wardrobe that mirrored the gradual healing of their hearts, guiding the bereaved on a visible journey from darkness back to light, almost literally.

However, before delving into the haute couture of death, an ensemble known as the 'widow's weeds', we need to establish the 'Classifications of Mourning' a woman had to follow upon the death of a loved one. These were divided into three mourning categories/stages – 'full/deep', 'second' and 'half' – and were determined by her relationship to the deceased and her socio-economic position in society.

William Harker's Jet Manufacturing in Alders Waste on Church Street, Whitby, UK

FULL/DEEP MOURNING:
this typically lasted a year and a day. Women wore all-black clothing crafted from non-reflective, matte fabrics like bombazine, crepe and wool. Jewellery was limited to stones like jet, a black, shiny gemstone.

SECOND MOURNING:
this lasted about six months, allowing for the introduction of small amounts of grey or purple and a less strict use of materials

HALF MOURNING:
this period lasted three to six months, during which women could incorporate a broader range of colours, such as grey, lavender and white, often in more elaborate designs.

The duration for which a woman wore mourning attire could seem as though it were decreed by a judge meting out sentences.

The death of a husband – a year and a day
(or as much as the rest of her life)
The death of a child – 6–12 months
The death of a parent – 6–12 months
The death of a grandparent – 6 months

Five female family members in mourning wear in response to the death of someone close to them.

Deep Mourning enveloped women in the sombre hues of loss. Black dominated every aspect of their attire, from the dresses and bonnets devoid of ornamentation to the veils that shrouded their faces in privacy. Even their gloves, shoes, fans, shawls and accessories whispered the language of sorrow in muted black.

As time softened the sharp edges of grief, women transitioned into the stage of Second Mourning. This phase allowed for a gentle reintroduction of adornment. The oppressive veils and crepe were set aside, making room for intricately designed jewellery and dresses accented with tasteful white trims. This subtle shift marked a turning point, a relaxing of the strict codes of bereavement.

Eventually, the mourning attire lightened further, embracing the softer shades of lilac, purple and grey as women entered the final stage, known as light mourning. This stage was a visual testament to the gradual return of colour into the lives of the bereaved, symbolizing a reawakening and a gentle embrace of life's continuing cycle. Each stage of mourning, with its prescribed fashions, provided a structured path through grief, offering women a way to outwardly express their inner journey of healing.

The classic portrait of Queen Victoria in full mourning wear and a lifeless gaze of sorrow.

HEART ON YOUR SLEEVE

One of the most iconic examples of mourning fans was the black lace fan. Elegant and sombre, it embodied the aesthetic of mourning attire. The lace often featured involuted scrollwork patterns and floral motifs, symbolizing the ephemeral nature of life and the beauty of memory. The handles of these fans were typically made of ebony or other dark wood. When unfurled, the lace fan provided a veil-like effect, allowing the mourner a degree of privacy and protection from the outside world.

If one were financially fortunate and had a flare for the dramatic, they would be seen around the city with their face hidden behind a fan adorned with black feathers. These fans were usually large and opulent, made from ostrich or marabou feathers dyed in deep black hues. The soft, flowing plumes symbolized the mourner's sorrow, their gentle movement mirroring the ebb and flow of grief. The handles of such fans were often made of polished ebony, with occasional inlays of mother-of-pearl or silver. Feather fans were particularly favoured with evening wear; the dramatic appearance complemented the more formal aspects of mourning dress.

Paper fans also played a role in Victorian mourning customs, often decorated with printed designs that carried symbolic meaning. Common motifs included weeping willows, urns and angels, all being traditional symbols of mourning and the afterlife. The fans' spines were made of black-stained wood or blackened bone, starkly contrasting the lighter paper. Some fans were hand painted with scenes of mourning, such as a widow in a graveyard or a sorrowful maiden by a tomb, transforming it into a miniature work of art that conveyed the depth of the mourner's loss.

Silk mourning fans were another exquisite accessory. These fans were typically made from black silk, sometimes adorned with subtle embroidery in silver or dark hues. The handles were crafted from materials like jet or tortoiseshell, chosen for their dark, reflective qualities. Silk fans were lightweight, elegant and particularly popular among the upper classes, who valued the material's refined and understated beauty in their mourning attire.

Black crepe, known for its distinctive crinkled texture, was a popular material for mourning garments. Fans made from black crepe were simple yet deeply symbolic, their texture and appearance representing the weight of grief. The handles of these fans were often left unadorned and made from plain black wood or bone, emphasizing the austerity and solemnity of the person's mourning.

These fans were more than mere accessories; they provided both comfort and a tangible connection to the memory of the departed, and perpetuated the act of mourning into a public ritual.

BEHIND THE VEIL

Historians have provided a few theories on the true meaning of wearing the veil. Some say it was socially and ethically inappropriate to have any public show of emotion and veils were a way for women to hide their grief-laden tears. Others feel the black veil was symbolic since it allowed very little light to penetrate, thus symbolizing the removal of light from the widow's life. In an odd twist, some women used the mourning veil as protection against unwanted male advances, with veiled women in black being seen as sexually appealing at the time.

For the first three months of mourning, the widow wore a black weeping veil, usually silk, draped over her face and upper torso. However, it was not uncommon to witness a black spectre floating down the road, with a veil cascading down the entire length of her body.

Some women felt their grief demanded a more intense lamentation and wore veils made of crepe, which were very heavy, suffocating and challenging to see through. It must be mentioned that in addition to the garments being black, they needed to have as little reflective quality as possible. To achieve this characteristic, the veils were treated with a combination of arsenic, chromium, benzene, potassium dichromate or copper chloride. All are highly toxic chemicals and when wet, when perhaps the widow was caught out in the rain, the dyes would inevitably separate from the material and leech into the wearer's skin, leading to various painful dermatological conditions.

Countess Olivia in William Shakespeare's *Twelfth Night*. A grieving beauty, is depicted in mourning dress, raising a black veil to show her face at last.

In more acrid environments, the dyes would dry and shed tiny dust particles, and long-term wearing of the mourning veil had been known to result in respiratory problems, vision disorders and even blindness. When a few cases of veil-induced death occurred as a direct result of the long-term inhalation of toxic dust, articles began to appear in medical journals and newspapers debating the pernicious side effects of mourning veils. When the woman reached Second

Mourning, the veil was moved to the back of the head, off the face and a black crepe bonnet was the accepted chapeau.

Men largely escaped these traumas, however. They were, after all, the family's breadwinners and their mourning period was shorter. In fact, it was so brief that the day following the burial, they were expected to return to work. Unlike the many components that constituted a 'widow's weeds', a man's mourning attire was a black suit and a veil-like stretch of crepe called a 'weeper' acted as a band on his silk black top hat. The width of the crepe denoted his relationship to the deceased. In addition to the weeper, men's mourning fashions could include mourning gloves, black armbands or a black ribbon on the lapel.

DEADLY FASHION

The conventional image of Victorian-era mourning attire is often one of uniform sombreness: black garments that covered a woman from her neck to her feet, reflecting a strict adherence to the codes of decorum and modesty. However, this depiction simplifies the intricate relationship between mourning customs and fashion, particularly among the upper echelons of society, where high fashion significantly influenced the design of mourning wear. Even when Queen Victoria adopted mourning dress after the death of her husband, Prince Albert, in 1861, her attire still reflected the prevailing fashionable silhouettes of the time, such as the crinoline, and later the bustle, popular at different parts of her long reign and mourning period.

In the book *The Ladies' and Gentlemen's Etiquette: A Complete Manual of the Manners and Dress of American Society* (1877), Eliza Bisbee Duffy clearly defines that the acceptable fabrics suited for deep mourning are serge (heavy wool), bombazine (wool and silk), alpaca fibre, Delaine or *de laine* (fine combing wool), merino (thinner/softer wool) and crepe or silk for collars, cuffs, bonnets and veils. These materials were not only chosen for

Prime Minister William Ewart Gladstone, his wife and daughter dressed in full mourning.

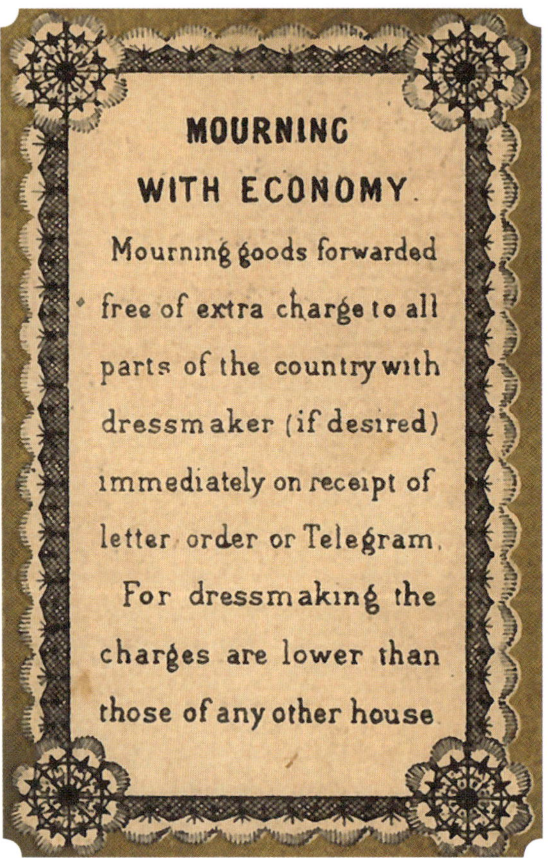

A small two-sided advertising card for a company specializing in affordable mourning clothes.

their sombre appearance but also for their ability to convey a sense of prestige and delicacy. In contrast, those of lower economic status typically wore less expensive materials like cotton or wool.

Moreover, the detailing on the mourning garments of the upper class was often intricate and subtly lavish. While embellishments were generally frowned upon in deep mourning, as the mourning period progressed, it became acceptable to introduce more decorative elements to personal apparel. This could include jet beads (a type of lignite coal often used in mourning jewellery due to its dark, glossy appearance) sewn into gowns to add a discreet yet opulent touch. Mourning dresses might also feature flounces and ruffles made of the same fabric as the main body of the garment, positioned in a manner that maintained modesty yet added a layer of sophisticated design.

To complete her ensemble, a widow would often select accessories that not only adhered to the strict codes of mourning etiquette but subtly expressed her loss, enduring love and, of course, her sense of high fashion.

Mourning fans were unique in their design and purpose. Typically made of black fabric or lace and often adorned with ostrich feathers and sombre motifs, such as weeping willows or cypress trees, these fans were not just practical tools for alleviating the heat but also symbols of widowhood and loss. Women used them discreetly to communicate their emotional state or to signal during social interactions without speaking. There is a whole language connected to fans.

Gloves were another crucial element, typically dyed black to match the rest of the ensemble. They were often made of kid leather or silk and were expected to be worn at all times in public. Mourning shoes were similarly fashioned in black, often made of satin or kid leather. The soles were also black, ensuring that no part of the mourner's attire drew unnecessary attention or appeared inappropriately ornate.

Mourning parasols followed the same strict colour scheme. Beyond their practical use as sun protection, these parasols were visual markers of a woman's bereavement status. Like the fans, gloves and veils, the accessories chosen helped maintain a barrier between a woman as the grieving widow and the outside world . . . the world of the living.

Even the smallest details were considered during mourning, and handkerchiefs were no exception. Typically edged in black, they were used not just for practical purposes but also as a discreet display of mourning etiquette.

SYMBOLISM – JET, ONYX AND HUMAN HAIR

Victorian-era mourning jewellery embodies a unique cultural approach to remembrance and grief, distinguishing itself significantly from the motifs found in the Middle Ages. During the Victorian period, mourning jewellery evolved into a profound expression of love and loss.

One of the most distinctive features of Victorian mourning jewellery is its use of specific materials, notably dark stones such as jet, onyx and black glass, and, remarkably, incorporating the hair of the deceased. This latter practice particularly highlights the period's focus on personal connection and sentimentality. Hair, a direct physical link to the deceased, was often woven intricately into brooches, rings and bracelets, sometimes accompanied by inscriptions or initials.

The design and symbolism in Victorian mourning jewellery also marked a departure from earlier traditions. Unlike in the Middle Ages, where death was often depicted through stark and somewhat morbid symbols (skulls, skeletons and coffins), known as 'memento mori' – discussed later in the book – the Victorian approach was more subdued and symbolic. Images such as weeping willows, urns and clasped hands were popular, symbolizing sorrow, remembrance and eternal love. These symbols were not just decorative; they conveyed a coded language understood by those within Victorian society who had a more romanticized view of death, seeing it as a gentle sleep rather than a grim end.

Although collectors of Victoriana wish it were true, Victorian tear catchers, small vials purportedly used to collect mourners' tears, lack credible historical evidence. While sentimental Victorian mourning practices existed, tear catchers likely originated from a misinterpretation of ancient Roman lachrymatories. These vessels were for holding perfumes or oils, not tears. The myth perpetuates due to its intriguing narrative, yet lacks substantiated historical grounding amid genuine Victorian mourning customs.

A wealthy widow in Second Mourning is covered in silken satin and a bonnet.

A widow stands for a portrait with the famous photographer Pierre-Louis Pierson.

DOLLARS IN DEATH

As the popularity of mourning grew, enterprising individuals saw an opportunity to turn grieving into big business. Some attribute its commercialization, in this era, primarily to Queen Victoria who remained in mourning for her prince consort from 1861 until her death in 1901. Her extended public display of grief set a social precedent that elevated mourning practices to new heights, leading to an increased demand for special attire and creating a booming industry in clothing and related apparel. Small shops and large department stores began offering sections specializing in appropriate garments and accessories. The use in jewellery of the lustrous gemstone jet, for example, became so popular that the quaint town of Whitby, on England's North Yorkshire coast, saw its economy significantly bolstered by the demand. The area was a significant source of jet, formed during the Jurassic era from the fossilised wood of the Araucaria tree. By the 1870s, demand had outstripped supply, however, and the gemstone was imported into Britain from Spain.

A Victorian-era cabinet photograph shows a woman dressed in mourning clothes flanked by funeral flower arrangements.

Mourning etiquette books, which were widely circulated to guide the bereaved through the complex social rules, flew off the shelves. *The Queen's Regulations for Mourning*, and manuals by authors like Mrs Beeton, detailed the length of mourning periods appropriate for different relations, the suitable attire for each stage and the socially acceptable behaviour during grief. The widespread distribution of these guides helped standardize mourning practices across the various social classes in Britain, turning what previously had been personal grief in the private sphere into a public duty. ❀

CHAPTER IV

BRUSHES *with* MORTALITY

VICTORIAN ART IN THE SHADOW OF DEATH

THE GOOD DEATH

No facet of society could escape the pall of death that hung over the Western world during the nineteenth century. The constant reminder of one's mortality can be witnessed through the fine art and music of the time. Victorian-era art often mirrored society's complex attitudes towards death and mourning. In England and Wales, between 1851 and 1910, a staggering four million people died from tuberculosis, equating to 22 per cent to 11 per cent of the population based on the rising populace over the 60-year span. Also known as 'consumption', 'phthisis' or the 'white plague' with more than a third of those aged between 15 to 34, and a half between 20 to 24.[8] The result landed the disease with another moniker: 'the robber of youth'.

In the United States, things were not faring much better, with TB accounting for nearly one out of every ten deaths in that same period. The disease could claim a generation of a family, taking child upon child until the nest was empty. Author Caroline Seabury notes in her diary that in the 1850s, seven of her eight siblings were taken from her by the disease.[9] No one was insulated from it, with many notable victims, including James Monroe, 5th president of the United States, composer Frédéric Chopin, naturalist and author Henry David Thoreau, gunslinger John Henry 'Doc' Holliday and playwright Anton Chekhov.

Despite its cruel and deadly nature, it became a romanticized disease, its long, drawn-out death thought of as a way of easing into the afterlife. It thus received another nickname, 'the good death'. Before they died, some believed that the suffering inflicted upon the tuberculosis victim had positive consequences, such as heightened sensitivity. British poet Lord Byron did not help matters when he allegedly said to a friend, 'I should like to die of a consumption.' 'Why?' countered his friend. 'Because the ladies would all say, "Look at that poor Byron, how interesting he looks in dying!"'[10] His wish was not granted, however, and he would die instead of sepsis. And it wasn't just literary figures who used the bacteria *Mycobacterium tuberculosis* as their muse; artists from all facets claimed her as their own, too.

Richard Tennant Cooper, *Syphilis*, gouache on board, c.1912. Syphilis and its associations with the sins of the flesh portrays the woman as a sultry omen.

TUBERCULOSIS AS A MUSE

This macabre attitude to TB is palpable in the works of the Pre-Raphaelite Brotherhood, a secret group of English painters, poets and critics founded in 1848. Fine artists like Dante Gabriel Rossetti, John Everett Millais, John William Waterhouse and William Holman Hunt often depicted women 'romantically' in various states of wasting away from the white plague. Pale, skeletal figures with delicately flushed cheeks became celebrated as the epitome of femininity, linking fragility indelibly with beauty in states of languor or death, shrouded in rich, symbolic imagery.

The watercolour by Pierre Georges Jeanniot of *Lady of the Camellias* based on the *La Dame aux Camélias* by Alexandre Dumas fils (1902) has the classic elements of the good death. The woman is reclined in a posture of weakness, one arm listlessly hanging by her side and the other draped across her chest. She woefully gazes back at her lover with vacant eyes. However, despite this morbid posturing, the image is interpreted as one of beauty, grace and eroticism.

Pierrre Georges Jeanniot, *Lady of the Camellias (La Dame aux Camélias)*, 1902.

This pursuit of a 'macabre chic' beauty led some women to use arsenic as a cosmetic despite its known toxicity. Arsenic, as we have already discussed in the previous chapter, was prized for its reputed ability to impart a pale, translucent skin tone, highly coveted as it symbolized beauty and social status. Marketed in various forms, including arsenic wafers and complexion powders, it was used to achieve the desirable 'arsenic complexion'. The use of arsenic-based products was a dangerous practice, as prolonged exposure could lead to severe health consequences, including organ damage and, ultimately, death.

Edvard Munch's *The Sick Child* (1885–6) captures the moment before his sister Johanne Sophie's death from tuberculosis at the age of 15. The artist's mother had also succumbed to the disease when he was five. Over the next 40

The Sick Child, one of six series by Edvard Munch (1863-1944), oil on canvas. (c.1886).

years, Munch relived his sister's death in six paintings and lithographs. *The Sick Child* depicts a pallid Sophie on her deathbed, supported by a large white pillow, supported by a dark-haired woman, head bowed, likely her aunt, Karen, both women visibly marked by grief. Sophie's haunted expression and the ominous black curtain symbolize the pervasive presence of death. Munch suffered lifelong guilt of surviving tuberculosis when he was a child, while his sister died of it.

Although not a member of the Pre-Raphaelite Brotherhood, William Lindsay Windus's 1858 *Too Late* is a poignant and evocative painting that captures the emotional depth and narrative richness characteristic of the artistic movement. When this painting was initially exhibited, it was with a quotation from the Tennyson's poem which had inspired it, 'Come not when I am dead'.

In *Too Late*, Windus presents a heart-wrenching scene of a woman in the throes of consumption and emotional despair, held by her rosy-cheeked, healthy companion in a purple dress. Her physical frailty is depicted with painstaking realism – sunken eyes and hollow cheeks. She stands as a symbol of literal lovesickness, her body supported by a crutch, emphasizing her vulnerability and the severity of her condition.

The interaction between the characters is charged with intense emotion. The woman, facing her beloved, conveys a mix of accusation and sorrow through her haunting gaze. Her lover, in contrast, appears overwhelmed by guilt and regret for the pain he caused as a result of abandoning his fiancé only to return months later and find her ravaged by consumption. He turns his face away, unable to meet her eyes. This dynamic captures a tragic moment of realization – his return has come too late to salvage their love or her health.

There is no such subtly in R. Cooper's watercolour (c.1912) of a sickly young woman seated on a balcony, her frail form wrapped in blankets, depicting the devastating impact of tuberculosis. Commissioned by Henry S.

Wellcome – and part of the Wellcome Collection – the allegory shows a balcony setting, an open yet confining space, reflecting the paradox of the patient seeking fresh air – a common, albeit ineffective, treatment for TB – while trapped by the illness. The young woman's pallor and fragile demeanour, as she watches the scene, emphasize her deteriorating health.

Looming ominously above her is the personification of death, shown as a ghostly skeleton clutching a scythe and an hourglass. This figure, a classic symbol of mortality, underscores the relentless and inescapable nature of the disease. Traditionally associated with the Grim Reaper, the scythe represents the imminent end of life. At the same time, the hourglass signifies the fleeting passage of time, heightening the urgency and despair of the scene.

Cooper's use of watercolour enhances the painting's delicate and ephemeral quality, mirroring the fragile existence of those afflicted by the disease. The soft, muted tones create a melancholic atmosphere, emphasizing the young woman's quiet suffering. Through this poignant portrayal, Cooper not only documents the physical toll of tuberculosis but also captures the emotional and psychological weight borne by its victims.

William Lindsay Windus, *Too Late*, 1858.

TRAGIC BEAUTY

One poem by Alfred, Lord Tennyson, 'The Lady of Shalott', written in 1832, catalyzed two evocative paintings of this period. In John William Waterhouse's 1888 version rendered in sombre tones, it portrays the Lady, sitting in her boat, drifting towards her death. The background is a hauntingly serene landscape, while the foreground is a chaotic mix of live and dying reeds. On the end of the boat are three candles, which symbolize life. Two of the candles are extinguished, indicating that death is soon to come. Alongside are a crucifix,

The Lady of Shalott, John William Waterhouse (1849-1917), oil on canvas, 1888.

rosary and funerary symbols representing sacrifice and martyrdom. At the very tip of the boat hangs a funeral lantern. Waterhouse's meticulous brushstrokes and the ethereal glow that envelops the Lady create a haunting and heartbreakingly beautiful scene, reflecting the era's romanticization of tragic heroines.

In William Holman Hunt's *The Lady of Shalott*, the artist belaboured for nearly two decades (1886-1905) to bring to life his interpretation of Tennyson's poem. Hunt's version emphasizes the moment of the Lady's decision to leave her tower, fully aware of the curse that will lead to her death. The painting's rich, symbolic details and vibrant colours create a vivid and foreboding atmosphere. Here, the Lady is isolated in a tower and subject to a curse that tells her she cannot look at Camelot except in her mirror. The central idea is that she is restricted and unable to pursue something she wants. Surrounded by the tapestry she has woven, the Lady gazes into a mirror that reflects the outside world, symbolizing her yearning and isolation. The broken loom threads indicate the moment of her defiance, suggesting her impending doom. The landscape visible through the window contrasts the confined, shadowy interior, emphasizing the Lady's entrapment. The price of looking out the window at Camelot, as the Lady finds out, is death. The artist depicts the tragic tale of a cursed woman doomed to view the world only through a mirror, ultimately leading to her demise.

The painting *Ophelia* (1851–2) by John Everett Millais, inspired by Shakespeare's *Hamlet* is enveloped by pain and misery, figuratively and literally. In the painting, *Ophelia* is seen floating down the river moments before drowning. The lush, natural surroundings contrast starkly with

Ophelia, Sir John Everett Millais, oil on canvas. (c.1852).

Ophelia's lifelessness, emphasizing the tenuousness of life. Millais's attention to botanical accuracy was achieved through painstaking studies of plants along the Hogsmill River. In fact, Millais completed painting the scenery before beginning work on the central figure. The flowers that appear on Ophelia's body are also highly symbolic. The chain of violets around Ophelia's neck symbolizes faithfulness, chastity or death. The pansies on her legs represent unrequited love and the red poppy – although never mentioned by Shakespeare – signifies death.

The model seen floating in the water is Elizabeth Siddal. At 19, she became part of the Pre-Raphaelite circle and quickly gained fame as the model for Millais's *Ophelia*. Unfortunately, to achieve the desired effect, Millais had Siddal lie in a bathtub filled with water for hours on end, ultimately leading to her becoming severely ill.

Siddal developed a passionate and tumultuous relationship with poet and artist Dante Gabriel Rossetti. She became his primary muse and model, inspiring many of his works. However, Siddal was not only a muse; she was also a talented artist and poet. Encouraged by Rossetti, she developed her skills in painting and drawing, creating poignant works that often reflected her inner turmoil and delicate sensibilities. Her poetry, characterized by its melancholic beauty and introspective themes, further showcased her creative depth.

In 1860, Siddal and Rossetti married, but their union was marred by her fragile health and his infidelities. Struggling with various ailments, including an addiction to laudanum, Siddal's health deteriorated. She gave birth to a stillborn daughter in 1861, a loss that deepened her despair and, arguably, led to her life being cut tragically short when she died from a laudanum

Beata Beatrix, Rossetti, c.1870. The painting depicts Beatrice Portinari from Dante Alighieri's 1294 poem 'La Vita Nuova' at the moment of her death.

overdose on 11 February 1862, at the age of 32. After her death, Rossetti created *Beata Beatrix* (1863–c.70) depicting his late wife in a death-like trance. Images of opium poppies in the painting hint at Siddal's laudanum overdose a nd her untimely death.

Gotch Thomas Cooper's painting *Death The Bride* (1895) depicts a young, ethereal and ghostly bride, clad in a nondescript gown, a flowing black veil and a crown of flowers. Her slight smile suggests an acceptance of her fate, as if she is both a bride and a personification of death. The dark, muted background enhances the bride's pale complexion, creating a stark contrast that emphasizes her otherworldly presence. The bride stands in a field of poppies, a not-so-subtle hint at impending doom. Laudanum is prepared by dissolving extracts from the opium poppy, and it was the drug of choice for medicinal reasons and for committing suicide.

GONE TOO SOON: YOUTH AND MORTALITY IN VICTORIAN ART

Sir Luke Fildes's *The Doctor* (1891) presents a different yet equally compelling narrative of mortality. The painting shows a doctor attentively watching over a sick child, his expression a mix of hope and concern. This intimate scene reflects the era's anxieties about illness, particularly the high infant mortality rates that plagued Victorian society. Fildes, who experienced personal tragedy with the loss of his own son, channels his grief into this work, creating a powerful image of compassion and the transient nature of our existence.. The warm light that bathes the scene contrasts with the sombre subject matter, representing the delicate balance between life and death.

Henry Wallis's *The Death of Chatterton* (1856) illustrates the romanticized view of youthful death that captivated the Victorian imagination.

The Death of Chatterton, Henry Wallis, oil on panel (c.1856).

The painting shows the young poet Thomas Chatterton, who committed suicide at 17, lying lifeless on his bed. Wallis's use of vibrant colours and dramatic lighting creates a sense of tragic beauty, highlighting the notion of the tortured artist. The work reflects the Victorian idealization of young geniuses cut down in their prime. This theme resonated deeply in a society fascinated by the connections between creativity, madness and mortality.

Charles Spencelayh's painting *His First Grief*, completed in 1910, captures the universal experience of loss through the eyes of a child. Spencelayh, known for his meticulous attention to detail and ability to portray human emotion, uses his skills to delve into the theme of grief with a deep sensitivity.

The painting depicts a young boy in a domestic setting, holding a dead bird, his expression one of profound sadness. His tattered clothes reveal that his family is not one of means, and the loss of his pet is not easily replaced by the childhood comforts of the wealthy. His small, slumped, solitary figure contrasts with the empty spaces around him, emphasizing his isolation in the face of grief.

Spencelayh's use of lighting focuses on the boy's face, drawing the viewer's attention to his expression, which is the emotional centre of the work. The artist's choice of dark colours contributes to the melancholic atmosphere, enhancing the thematic depth of the painting. *His First Grief* invites viewers to reflect on the inevitable, often premature, introduction to the complexities of emotional pain as a result of death.

His First Grief, Charles Spencelayh (c.1910).

ETHEREAL EROTICISM

Luis Ricardo Falero's painting *Vision of Faust* (c.1878), also known as *The Departure of the Witches*, intricately blends themes of the supernatural and the erotic, aligning with Victorian interests in the spirit world and a socially acceptable form of voyeurism during a period of repressed sexuality.

The painting draws inspiration from Goethe's *Faust*, specifically the Walpurgis Night scene shown by Mephisto to Faust at Blocksberg, in the Harz mountains of Germany. Traditionally a celebration of the Spring Equinox by Nordic and Celtic cultures, Walpurgis Night was later reimagined as a gathering of witches with Satan.

In *Vision of Faust*, Falero portrays this encounter as not a physical event but a haunting vision. The scene is charged with eroticism, with provocatively posed nudes and figures in overtly sexual interactions amid visions of horror and darkness, including monsters and the dead. The composition spirals, continuously drawing the viewer's gaze around the tempestuous sky scene, from the subdued witches and devils in the background to the vivid centre. Central to the image is a woman who looks directly at the viewer, her gaze blending allure and menace, suggesting that the viewer is not just an observer but a participant in this sinister yet seductive tableau.

Luis Ricardo Falero, *Vision of Faust*, oil on canvas, c.1878.

Amid the perfect storm of deadly epidemics, an intense societal obsession with mourning, and the looming threat of faith eroding in the face of relentless industrialization, Victorian-era fine artists 'fortunately' found themselves enveloped by the dark inspiration that arises from grappling with the boundaries of life and death. This sombre yet fertile landscape birthed some of the era's most hauntingly evocative imagery, capturing a society's desperate struggle with the fragile nature of human existence. ꕥ

CHAPTER V

CITY *of the* DEAD

FAMILY PLOTS TO THE NECROPOLIS

GRAVE CONCERNS

The Victorian era saw a transformation in the design and function of cemeteries. Previously, burials were typically conducted in churchyards, however, due to the rapid urbanization and population growth of many cities in Europe and the United States, and increasing mortality rates, these hallowed grounds became overcrowded and unsanitary.

In the first half of the nineteenth century, London's population surged from under a million, in 1801, to nearly 2.5 million by 1851. Although the Magnificent Seven garden cemeteries of Kensal Green, West Norwood, Highgate, Abney Park, Brompton, Nunhead and Tower Hamlets existed in London, all built between 1833 and 1841, the demand for gravesites was not being met.

To manage the overflow, the oldest graves were regularly exhumed to make room for new burials. This practice led to decaying corpses contaminating the water supply, contributing to frequent outbreaks of cholera, smallpox, measles and typhoid. In addition, the public health policy was primarily influenced by the miasma theory, previously discussed, which held that airborne particles were the primary spreaders of disease. The foul odours and the health risks from stacked bodies and rotting exhumed corpses caused significant public outcry.

In response to the crisis, a Royal Commission was established, in 1842, to investigate. The commission concluded that London's burial grounds were so overcrowded that digging a new grave without disturbing an existing one was impossible. Yet, the commission was in no rush to solve this 'deadly problem'. Although it did develop the Cemeteries Clause Act,[11] which provided guidelines for establishing and running commercial cemeteries, it wasn't until 1848 that natural ground was broken – literally and figuratively. The act was delayed due to strong opposition from the Church of England, concerns over church-state separation, social anxieties about burial practices, and complex legal issues regarding land ownership. Ultimately, the biggest resistance came from those seeking to preserve the Church's control over burial practices and churchyard burials. Between 1848 and 1849, a cholera epidemic ripped through England, killing 53,000 people in England with 14,601[12] in London alone, completely overwhelming the burial system. Bodies were left stacked in heaps awaiting burial, and even relatively recent graves were exhumed to make way for new burials.

The first Public Health Act was given Royal Assent on 31 August 1848. This act laid the groundwork for public health measures and the beginning of a legislative process that would establish public cemeteries throughout the United Kingdom. This rethinking of cemeteries led to the rise of the Victorian garden cemetery. Although the Magnificent Seven were initially designed not only to house the dead of a growing London population but also to do so in a pleasant environment, they could not keep up with the frantic demand of an ever-expanding/dying population. The Victorian

The gloomy entrance to the Necropolis, Glasgow.

garden movement addressed these issues by creating spacious, landscaped cemeteries with picturesque landscapes, winding paths and elaborate monuments outside the city limits. These cemeteries were burial places and yet served as public parks where people could visit, reflect and enjoy the surroundings, epitomizing Victorian aesthetics and a reverence for the dead.

One of the first 'old style' cemeteries to feel the wrath of the new commission was Cross Bones Cemetery, which had its wrought iron gates locked in 1853. A notorious cemetery in one of London's dirtiest and most dangerous slums, Cross Bones was the final resting place for most of the women of ill repute who worked the South Bank and were forbidden from burial in consecrated church grounds because of their sinful ways. However, it was said that the bodies didn't stay buried for long due to the cemetery's proximity to Guy's Hospital and its need for teaching cadavers.

Urbanization, rapid population growth, and all the infrastructure problems that come with them, were not exclusive to England. Other European countries and the United States faced these issues and were forced to confront them. In fact, the US adopted the cemetery as a peaceful escape for the dead and their families in the 1830s, with the Rural Cemetery Movement, influenced by Romanticism, natural elements featuring predominantly in, and important to, their design and aspect.

Mount Auburn Cemetery in Cambridge,

Massachusetts, was established in 1831, and the first example of such places, inspiring the creation of similar cemeteries across the country. Designed to be serene and beautiful, these 'rural' burial grounds contrasted starkly with the crowded and grim churchyards of the recent past. They became popular destinations for recreation and contemplation, blending the concepts of public parks and gravesites. The Parisian Père Lachaise Cemetery, established in 1804, with its park-like design and monumental tombs, became a prototype for British and American garden cemetery design. Reformists and the public supported the Rural Cemetery Movement not just for the aesthetic benefits of such burial parks, but because the dead did not have to be interred in overcrowded, unsanitary conditions, where they were liable to be uprooted. Finally, the dead could rest in peace in one picturesque place, where their families could visit them – and also have the prospect, one day, of joining them.

RESURRECTIONIST: THE DARK TRADE OF THE DEAD

Throughout the Western world, getting a grave dug was relatively easy. In addition to the church sexton who regularly doubled as the cemetery grave digger (before being US president, Abraham Lincoln dug graves when he was the sexton of his church), labourers, farmers, cement workers all moonlighted as gravediggers. In addition to this job, sometimes they would be called upon to participate in 'tapping' – hammering a pipe into the wooden casket in order to let the corpse gas that filled the coffin escape, preventing the coffin from exploding. But that issue only existed if the body stayed in place. While finding people to dig graves was not problematic, retaining those corpses in graves was.

The Victorian era was a time of advancement in medical science, particularly in anatomy and surgery. Medical schools required a steady supply of cadavers for dissection and research, but legal sources were limited. England's Anatomy Act of 1832 allowed unclaimed bodies from workhouses and hospitals to be used for medical research, but before that, medical schools and anatomists in England, the rest of Europe and the US relied heavily on grave robbers or 'body snatchers' to sell them corpses for dissection. Even esteemed institutions such as the Royal College of Surgeons in London were in constant need of cadavers and reportedly employed the services of these body snatchers. Anatomists, both famous and obscure, were willing to turn a blind eye to the source in order to further their understanding of human anatomy. The demand was so high that some medical practitioners even formed clandestine networks to ensure a steady supply. This unholy alliance between grave robbers and the medical community perpetuated this dark trade for decades.

These groups, also known as 'resurrectionists', were handsomely rewarded for

A Victorian-era engraving illustrating body snatchers stealing a corpse from the grave via the rope around the neck method.

their grisly work. Anatomists and medical schools paid between £2 and £10 per body, depending on the freshness and condition of the cadaver. To put this in perspective, £10 in the Victorian era would be equivalent to several months' wages for a labourer. The allure of easy money drew some of the same men who dug the graves in the day to return to the cemeteries under the cover of darkness to resurrect the dead. Some operated in small gangs, each member playing a crucial role, from the lookout to the digger. Yet the work was dangerous, grave robbers frequently attacked by anti-resurrectionists and those who disapproved of dissection.

Medical schools required a steady supply of cadavers for dissection and research, but legal sources were limited.

THE 'HOW TO' AND WHO'S WHO

Grave robbers spent most of their time making the grave area look undisturbed after the fact. The diggers sought a fresh grave since the dirt was easier to remove. A tarp was laid beside the grave to hold the earth. A vertical shaft was dug at the head of the grave, deep enough to reach the coffin. This minimized the amount of soil needed to be removed and allowed robbers to possibly avoid detection. Once the coffin was exposed, a crowbar or similar tool was used to smash open the top portion, place a rope around the corpse's neck or under its shoulders and slide the body up and out. They could then strip the body of its clothes and any valuables, toss the clothes back into the casket, refill the grave with earth and make the area appear untouched.

Grave robbing was a crime, but the penalties varied and were often lenient. Initially, the theft of a body was considered a misdemeanour rather than a serious crime. Technically, resurrectionists caught in the act faced fines, imprisonment or public whipping. In practice, the lack of stringent laws and the high demand for cadavers often led to light sentences, making the risk worth the reward for many.

Several grave robbers gained notoriety during the Victorian era. William Burke and William Hare, although more infamous for their murders than their body snatching, were integral to the dark trade. Operating in Edinburgh, they supplied 16 bodies, involving the murder of 15, to anatomist Dr Robert Knox before their capture in 1828. Hare turned king's evidence and testified against Burke. He went free but Burke received the maximum sentence. On the morning of 28 January 1829, Burke was hanged before a crowd estimated to have been up to 35,000. Enterprising residents of the nearby tenements, which offered prime views of the gallows, sold window spots for prices ranging from 5 to 20 shillings. The spectators, realizing Hare was not on the

A group of mortsafes, with both iron cages and cement slabs, in Cluny Old Kirkyard in Aberdeenshire, Scotland.

hangman's scaffold began to cheer, '*Hare, Hare! Where is Hare?*' and '*Hang Hare!*'[13]

In an ironic twist of fate, On 1 February 1829, Burke's body was publicly dissected by Professor Alexander Monro in the anatomy theatre of the university's Old College. The grim procedure lasted two hours, during which Monro grabbed a sheet of paper and famously dipped his quill into Burke's blood to write, '*This is written with the blood of Wm Burke, who was hanged at Edinburgh. This blood was taken from his head.*' Burke's skeleton was later donated to the Anatomical Museum of the Edinburgh Medical School, where it remains on display at the time of writing. His death mask and a book reportedly bound in his tanned skin can be seen at the Surgeons' Hall Museum. [14]

Other notorious resurrectionists included John Bishop, Thomas Williams and Michael Shields, members of the London Burkers. Bishop and his accomplices were responsible for the murder of several individuals and up to 1,000 resurrected bodies sold onto medical schools. Their reign of terror ended on 8 November 1831 when Richard Partridge, the demonstrator of anatomy at King's College School of Anatomy, declined to buy a cadaver. He contacted the police, not because he believed the body had been stolen, but rather that it showed no signs of being buried at all, leading him to believe the cadaver belonged to a murder victim. Williams and Shields were arrested and imprisoned: after confessing to the murders, they were sentenced to death sentence and were hanged at Newgate on 5 December 1831, before a horde reportedly of tens of thousands. Their bodies were removed the same night, Bishop to King's College and Williams to the Theatre of Anatomy in Windmill Street, The Haymarket, for dissection. In the following days, large crowds were allowed to view their remains.

GRAVES OF PROTECTION

Some relatives of the recently deceased employed a host of somewhat bizarre procedures to protect their loved ones' graves from body snatchers. One was to take measures even before the body reached the cemetery, some letting the body stay with them until it was so decomposed that it would have virtually no monetary value if it were unearthed. Other methods were to bury a body in a sealed metal coffin, line the inside of the grave with cement, place large, heavy slabs called 'mort stones' over the grave or construct iron cages, called 'mort safes', ensconced over the grave.

If a family had the financial means grand, above ground tombs or mausoleums were constructed to house entire families, often built with heavy stone and iron doors, making them more difficult to breach than traditional graves. Although at times, the ostentatiousness of the gravesite would indicate to grave robbers that it belonged to a wealthy "inhabitant" and therefore become a targeted site. Other deterrents included intricate locking mechanisms, iron bars across doors and windows and sometimes even booby

T. N. HOWELL,

Assignor to J., W., A. C. and J. W. RICE.

Grave Torpedo.

No. 9,719. **Reissued May 24, 1881.**

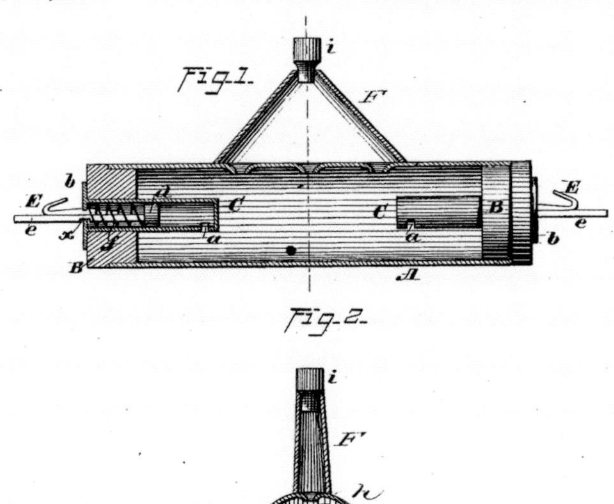

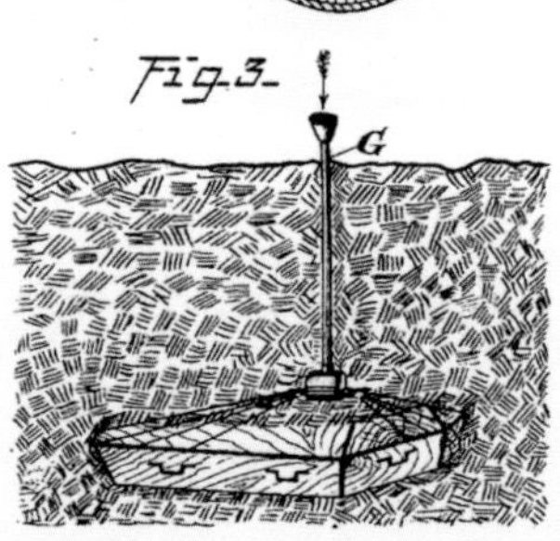

WITNESSES:

Jas. E. Hutchinson.

J. A. Rutherford

INVENTOR.

Thos. N. Howell,

by *James L. Norris.*

Attorney.

T.N. Clover submitted the patent for his version of the Grave Torpedo. (c.1881).

traps, such as spring-loaded mechanisms designed to injure intruders. Some mausoleums featured hidden compartments or false burial chambers, like the Egyptians, to confuse potential thieves.

The coffin torpedo and the coffin collars were two unique inventions. The coffin torpedo, patented in 1878 by Philip K. Clover in Columbus, Ohio, represents a fascinating intersection of engineering and funerary practices. Clover's innovation employed an explosive device concealed within the coffin and rigged to detonate if the grave was tampered with. It featured a spring-loaded percussion cap connected to a small explosive charge. When an attempt was made to open the coffin or disturb its contents, the torpedo would detonate, potentially maiming or killing the intruder.

A slightly less elaborate and dangerous method was the coffin collar. It involved slipping a heavy iron ring around the neck of the deceased and mounting the ring to a slab of thick wood, usually oak. This was secured to the base of the coffin with heavy bolts, rendering it impossible to remove the corpse without decapitating it, thus seriously reducing its value.

The layout and design of cemeteries also evolved to combat grave robbing. High walls, secure gates and limited entry points made it more difficult for robbers to gain access. Additionally, some cemeteries employed landscaping techniques, such as planting thorny bushes around graves, to create natural barriers.

These protective measures were generally exclusive to 'White' cemeteries in the United States and Europe. In the United States during the Victorian era, grave robbing had disproportionately affected African American cemeteries, with 'resurrectionists' targeting Black burial grounds with impunity. The racist underpinnings of society at the time, combined with a lack of legal protections for African American communities, made Black cemeteries particularly vulnerable to desecration.

Black cemeteries were seen as easy targets because African American families had little legal recourse to protect the graves of their loved ones. According to historical accounts, estimate as high as 50 per cent of the bodies exhumed for medical dissection in cities like Philadelphia and New York came from Black burial grounds, despite African Americans making up a significantly smaller percentage of the population. This discrepancy highlights the systemic racism of the period, where the bodies of Black cadavers were viewed as commodities for medical research, most often without consent.

One notorious example is the desecration of the Potter's Field in New York City, where Black bodies were routinely stolen for medical schools like Columbia and Bellevue Hospital. In 1788, the 'Doctors' Riot' erupted after medical students were caught exhuming bodies from a predominantly Black cemetery. The incident sparked outrage among Black communities, yet laws to protect their burial grounds remained lax for decades.

The grave robbing of Black cemeteries during the Victorian era also reflected broader societal attitudes towards race and death. African Americans' right to a dignified burial was systematically undermined. This violation of burial sites further fueled the trauma and indignity endured by Black families. [15]

This dark chapter in American history underscores the intersection of racism, science and the commodification of Black bodies. It serves as a stark reminder of the need for historical accountability and respect for the deceased, regardless of race or social status.

GRAVES OF HONOUR

Francis Chantrey, *The Sleeping Children*, marble.

Victorian tombstones and crypts were not just markers of death but were status symbols. They varied widely in style and size, reflecting the socio-economic status of the deceased and their family. 'It's all relative to the size of your steeple'[16] was determined by wealth, a truth that extended beyond life and into death during the nineteenth century.

Tombstones were often highly ornate, featuring elaborate carvings, statues and detailed inscriptions. The level of ornamentation was seen as a reflection of the deceased's family wealth and their alleged affection for the deceased. This style was significantly different from those of earlier periods, primarily in its complexity and symbolism. Pre-Victorian tombstones were typically much more simple, with basic inscriptions and minimal ornamentation. The Victorian emphasis on symbolism reflected the era's romanticized fascination with death and the Gothic revival happening in architecture.

Popular features that a family might choose to adorn their memorial masonry with, included:

ANGELS
representing guidance to heaven and protection

URNS
symbolizing the soul's immortality

DRAPERY
signifying mourning and the veil between life and death

WEEPING WILLOW TREES
denoting sorrow and mourning

OBELISKS
representing eternal life and remembrance

HANDS
symbolizing the deceased's ascent to heaven

ROSES
usually adorning young women's graves, and representing heavenly perfection and earthly passion

LAMBS
marking the grave of a small child

DOVES
symbolizing the Holy Spirit, purity and devotion

OPEN BOOKS
usually representing scholastic knowledge or scripture

CIRCLES
showing eternity and never-ending existence

CROSSES
signifying love, faith and goodness

CALVARY CROSS
denoting faith, hope and love

CELTIC CROSS
representing eternity

HANDSHAKE
an ancient symbol of devotion even at death, appearing on Greek, Etruscan and Roman funerary art

ANGEL
an agent of God, guardian of the dead

INVERTED TORCH
meaning life in the next realm or a life extinguished

An odd stereo card of three young girls visiting their mother's grave; unbeknownst to them, the spirit of their mother hovers over the children.

Several tombstone makers, known for their craftsmanship and contributions to funerary art, gained prominence during the Victorian era. James Forsyth was a renowned Scottish sculptor known for his work on Highgate Cemetery's Egyptian Avenue and other notable monuments. American sculptor William Wetmore Story was famous for the Angel of Grief monument in Rome, which became an iconic Victorian symbol of mourning. Sir Francis Chantrey was renowned for his funerary sculptures, which are marked by their serene and lifelike qualities, capturing the peaceful repose of the dead. His 1816 sculpture of the sleeping children in Lichfield Cathedral, in Staffordshire, depicting two young sisters who died in tragic circumstances, is an iconic example of this period's sculpture. The marble statue portrays the girls in slumber and encapsulates the Victorian romanticism of death.

GRAVES OF DREAD

For some of the dearly departed, the route from the parlour to the gravesite was interrupted by a short 'layover'. The fear of being buried alive was pervasive on both sides of the Atlantic. The paranoia stemmed from accounts of medical misdiagnosis, the lack of sophisticated methods to confirm death, sensationalist stories and the occasional real-life mishap. This fear led to the creation of specialized rooms and buildings designated for the dead to 'slumber' in. These spaces, often referred to as 'waiting mortuaries' or 'death houses', were designed to ensure that individuals were truly deceased before burial and to provide a place where bodies could be stored until there were clear signs of decomposition. This practice was more common in the United States, where larger, urban cemeteries could afford such measures.

Waiting mortuaries were equipped with various devices and methods to detect signs of life. These included glass panels for viewing the body's decomposition. Additionally, attendants were present to monitor the deceased for several days, checking for any signs of life. These places were usually situated near cemeteries or within hospital grounds, combining a sense of reverence with practical oversight.

These special mortuaries were not just functional spaces but masterpieces of interior design that blended sombre elegance with practicality. The interiors, adorned with furniture and drapery in rich, dark tones, created atmospheres of solemnity. The external architecture, often reflecting Gothic Revival styles, featured intricate details and imposing structures that conveyed a deep respect for the deceased and the gravity of the task.

These waiting mortuaries highlight the era's unique intersection of medical science, cultural practices and the profound anxiety surrounding death and burial. They testify to the period's meticulous approach to handling death, rooted in both compassion and fear.

This anxiety also led to the invention of 'safety coffins', designed to ensure that anyone mistakenly buried could signal for help. One typical design featured a bell attached to a string, which was placed in the hand of the deceased. If the person awoke, they could pull the string, thus ringing the bell and alerting those above ground. Some designs went further, incorporating complex systems of tubes and ropes that would raise a flag or open an air vent to provide oxygen. Another inventive design was the Bateson Revival Device, which included an air tube that allowed a buried person not just to breathe but to shout for help.

Despite the popularity of these designs, there is a lack of evidence to support they were widely used or that they ever successfully saved a life. Most safety coffins were marketed more on fear than practicality. Nonetheless, they highlight the Victorians' fascination with mortality and the lengths people would go to ensure a peaceful, final end. The safety coffins, in particular, testify to the Victorians' ingenuity driven by one of its most pervasive fear of being buried alive.

A SPEEDY PROCESS

William Guy, a professor of forensic medicine at King's College London, reviewed a case of a St Louis woman reported to have been revived during a ritual washing of her 'deceased' body. Guy commented that 'internment in this country is altogether too speedy; it should never take place till signs of putrefaction are observed'. In 1845, Guy published *Principle of Forensic Medicine in the UK* which established his ten principal signs of death.

CESSATION OF THE CIRCULATION
No pulse and no trace of a beating heart.

CESSATION OF RESPIRATION
Breathing has ceased. Most often, it is determined by whether a feather placed under the nose could be moved, a looking glass fogged up, or the water in a cup placed on the chest of the deceased would produce ripples.

THE FACIES OF HIPPOCRATES
The face takes on the characteristics of a sharp nose, sunken eyes, drawn-in ears with discoloured lobes, hard skin, pale complexion, relaxed lips and hollow cheeks.

THE STATE OF THE EYE
It loses its transparency and the globe-like state collapses.

STATE OF THE SKIN
Similar to elements in The Facies of Hippocrates, the skin develops a ghostly pallor and loss of elasticity.

INSENSIBILITY AND IMMOBILITY
The body is inert and does not respond to touch.

AN EXTERMINATION OF MUSCULAR IRRITABILITY
Even if the body/skin is stuck with a pin or sharp object, there is no muscle reaction.

EXTINCTION OF ANIMAL HEAT
A medical term that refers to the body heat produced by a living organism. There should be a considerable drop in temperature, depending on where the body was found, and it should be cold to the touch.

RIGIDITY
Now better known as rigor mortis, the joints stiffen, which reverses, and the limbs become mobile again after a period of time.

PUTREFACTION
Determined to be a sure sign of death, the stage at which the body experiences softening, bluish, greenish or brownish discolouration of the structures and omits a peculiar odour.[17]

William Guy's work was not the first forensic research to be published, Samuel Farr's *Elements of Medical Jurisprudence*, published in 1787, is considered to be the first text on forensic medicine written in the English language. Since then, there have been a number of other publications, most notably George Edward Male's *An Epitome of Juridicial or Forensic Medicine; For the Use of Medical Men, Coroners, and Barristers* published in 1816 and T.R. Beck's *Elements of Medical Jurisprudence* are all pretty similar in citing what happens to the human body as it passes through the stages of decomposition.

These works were embraced and helped give the medical community forensic guidelines and the laymen some peace of mind in confirming a deceased loved one was not going to be buried alive.

It was now time to streamline the trip from the morgue to the cemetery.

A ONE-WAY TICKET

The London Necropolis Company & National Mausoleum Company was established following a report by Sir Edwin Chadwick highlighting the health hazards posed by overcrowded burial grounds in London. Seizing an opportunity, the company purchased more than 2,000 acres of common land in 1852 in Woking, Surrey. Five hundred acres of the Brookwood site were set aside and when they were consecrated, two years later, it was the world's largest cemetery at the time.

The Brookwood burial site was strategically located about 40 miles southwest of London and was a significant departure from the gravesites found in London's urban centre. This location provided ample rolling countryside, ideal for constructing and landscaping a picturesque cemetery with park-like gardens. Completed in 1854, it was perfectly poised to cater to the needs of the nation's burgeoning population, now well over two million people, and its increasing number of deceased.

The London Necropolis Railway (LNR)

Examples of tickets issued by the Necropolis Railway for the three available classes.

decided to solve the problem of transporting the deceased and their mourners from the bustling city to its new cemetery by establishing a rail line that would get mourners and the deceased to and from the capital and Brookwood. A testament to Victorian resourcefulness, the LNR offered various services tailored to the era's needs. Trains departed from a dedicated station adjacent to Waterloo Station, exclusively designed for the LNR. It boasted waiting rooms, a mortuary and a chapel, where funeral services could be held before departure. The trains themselves were divided into first, second and third-class compartments. Each class offered different levels of comfort and privacy, ensuring accessibility for people of all financial backgrounds. Return tickets were issued for mourners, while single tickets were provided for the deceased.

There were also different classes of service for the cadavers. First-class tickets allowed families to choose the grave's exact location within the cemetery, while second – and third-class tickets offered less choice and more communal burial options. This stratification extended to the train cars, with first-class coffins in highly ornate train cars.

The rail route began at the Necropolis Station in London, ran through the southwestern suburbs, and terminated at two stations within Brookwood Cemetery. One station was for the Anglican populace, and the other served non-conformists. The service ran daily, except on Sundays and public holidays, and could transport multiple bodies and mourners in a single trip. The journey took about 40 minutes, offering a swift and dignified passage from the city to the serene countryside.

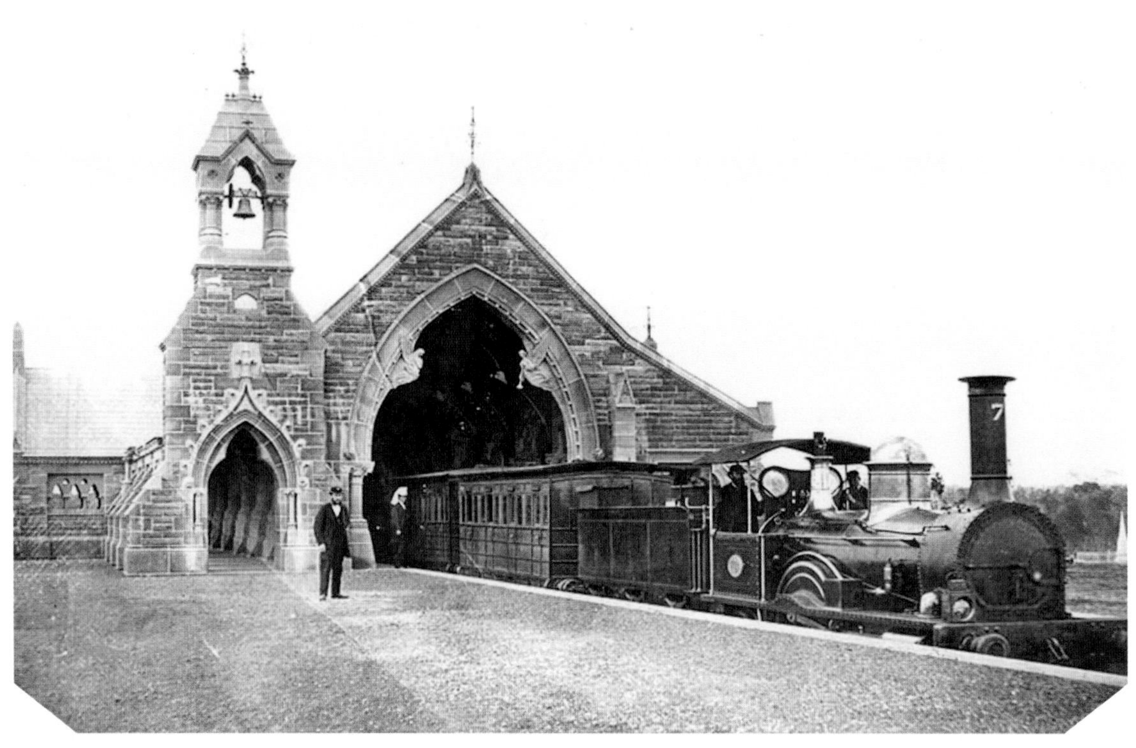

The entrance to the London Necropolis Railway was opened in November 1854 by the London Necropolis Company (LNC).

The Necropolis Train Company's station, Westminster Bridge Road, London, c.1903.

Initially, the LNR was a practical solution to London's burial issues since it was a fast and convenient way to shuttle mourners and the deceased out of the city and to the world's largest cemetery, but it faced competition from other cemeteries and the evolving funeral industry, and never achieved the popularity or the volume of business anticipated by its founders. Despite this, the railway operated for nearly a century, a testament to its unique role in Victorian society. The London Necropolis Railway ceased operations in 1941, primarily due to the heavy damage sustained by the German bombers during the Blitz of the Second World War and the subsequent shifts in burial practices.

Western customs surrounding the recognition of death and the burial of our loved ones have, in some respects, evolved dramatically over the last 200 years—yet in other ways, they have remained strikingly unchanged. While advances in medicine, technology, and societal attitudes have redefined the moment of death, our rituals for saying final goodbyes are still deeply rooted in traditions that have endured for centuries. It may take another 200 years, or more, to fully release the grip of these customs that continue to shape our farewells. ❀

The London Necropolis Railway Station, after an night air raid of World War II. (c.1941).

CHAPTER VI

CROSSING OVER

COMMUNICATING WITH THE GREAT BEYOND

THE BIRTHPLACE OF MODERN SPIRITUALISM

The Victorians were not just fascinated with the places where their loved ones were laid to rest, they also came to be obsessed with the idea that the spirit existed beyond matter, something that has captured the attention of civilizations throughout history. Spiritualism, a belief that the living could communicate with the dead, usually via mediums, became popular during this period.

Most historians trace the origins of modern spiritualism to Hydesville, a small town in Upstate New York. In March 1848, two young sisters, 15-year-old Margaretta (Maggie) and 11-year-old Catherine (Kate) Fox claimed that the house their family had recently moved into was haunted and that they could communicate with 'squatting' spirits by having them make otherworldly raps on the plaster walls and heavy wooden furniture. It's not clear how convinced Margaret was of her daughters' supposed gifts, however, she did agree to pose a simple question for the spirits to answer via her girls. When she asked, 'How many children do I have?' There was a brief moment of silence and then three distinct raps. Margaret did, indeed, have three children, daughters Leah, Maggie and Kate.

Convinced that this was not a benevolent spirit engaging in a simple guessing game, but something more 'demonic', Margaret sent her husband, John, to rouse the neighbours for help. A few hours later, the Foxes' bedroom was standing room only, with shocked neighbours reportedly witnessing paranormal aural activity via ongoing raps and knocking sounds – the language of the dead.

News of the strange happenings in the Fox residence quickly spread. And it wasn't long before what began as an innocent piece of mischief spiralled out of control, and the girls, who by now had added their older sister Leah's supernatural powers into the mix, found themselves caught up in a whirlwind of supernatural hysteria. Spiritualism was gaining popularity in the US and Europe, and the Fox sisters seemingly provided tangible evidence to many that such communications were possible.

Seances (from the Olde French seoir, 'to sit') where individuals attempted to communicate with the spirits became common, and people sought the sisters' guidance in contacting their departed loved ones. These guest spots at seances resulted in the sisters' fame soaring, and they embarked on a tour, showcasing their spiritual abilities in various cities across America. Crowds flocked to witness their seances, and they gained a devoted following. Maggie, Leah and Kate soon became celebrities of the spiritualist movement, attracting influential figures, including authors and scholars, eager to explore the mysteries of the afterlife.

The rise of the Fox sisters was not without controversy. Sceptics questioned the authenticity of their supernatural abilities and accusations

An illustration of the Fox sisters, including their oldest, Leah, who eventually became part of the spiritualist trio..

of fraud and deception cast a shadow over their reputation. Some suspected that the sisters may have manipulated the rapping sounds, while others believed it was all an elaborate hoax.

Despite these critics, the Fox sisters and a host of newly spawned mediums, necromancers, clairvoyants, channellers and mystics became the stars of the period, with high-profile devotees such as Abraham Lincoln's widow, Mary Todd. This phenomenon quickly became popular in Europe, especially in nineteenth-century England.

For almost four decades, the Fox sisters played to packed houses; they shrugged off the hecklers and haters, and many believe they played a part in the women's rights movement by giving a voice to women in an era where they, like children, were seen and not heard. They elevated the status of women entertainers within American popular culture, paving the way for numerous other spiritualists of their gender to achieve recognition and financial independence.

For almost four decades, the Fox sisters played to packed houses around the world.

PULLING BACK THE CURTAIN

Much of the lore surrounding the Fox sisters is conflicting stories of the who, what and where of their lives and, most notably, their professional decisions. Although, there is no debate that in 1888, at New York's Academy of Music, the 40-year run of the Fox sisters took a self-inflicted 180-degree turn when Maggie Fox, with Kate by her side, decided to confess that her and her sisters had perpetrated a scam on the public for over four decades. There are a few prevailing theories as to why Maggie finally confessed and demonstrated how they had created the rapping of the dead by 'snapping' the knuckles of their toes.

Some of the more popular suppositions are that as the fame of the Fox sisters grew, they faced increasing scrutiny and scepticism from the public and the press. They were constantly challenged to prove the authenticity of their abilities, which put them under immense pressure. Kate and Maggie may have felt stressed or guilty. By confessing, they could have sought closure and relief from the psychological burden of their actions.

Many believe Maggie's deep resentment toward her sister Leah who had publicly ridiculed their sister Kate, calling her a drunk and an unfit mother was a way for Maggie to exact revenge on Leah.

The Fox sisters' confession marked the end of their careers as spiritual mediums, and their legacy became a cautionary tale of the dangers of deception in the supernatural realm. Yet despite their downfall, the spiritualist movement continued to evolve and thrive, attracting new leaders who sought to explore the mysteries of the spirit world.

THE GHOSTS OF GREAT BRITAIN

It wasn't long before British devotees of the Fox sisters began holding seances in the candle-lit parlours of Londoners like Georgiana Eagle, James Burns and Florence Cook. These individuals had the faith of high-profile people like Queen Victoria and the writer Sir Arthur Conan Doyle.

Doyle, the creator of Sherlock Holmes, was a staunch supporter of mediums and spirit photography and even wrote a book entitled *The Coming of the Fairies* in which he discussed the Cottingley Fairies, seen reportedly in photographs that featured nine-year-old Frances Griffiths with four fairies and her cousin, sixteen-year-old Elsie Wright, with a dancing gnome. Doyle's support gave the photographs legitimacy, solidifying them as a cultural phenomenon. It wasn't until the 1980s that Elsie admitted the pictures were a hoax.

Doyle's second wife, Jean Leckie, was a self-proclaimed medium. She was a catalyst in the fracturing of Doyle and illusionist Harry Houdini's long friendship, which had begun through their shared interest in spiritualism. Yet, it would Houdini's desire to follow the truth and expose fraudulent mediums, whom he regarded as human leeches, that would cause friction in their relationship. While the Doyles were in Atlantic City, in 1922, Jean volunteered to contact Houdini's beloved deceased mother. Via automatic writing, Jean gave Houdini a series of messages from his mother that proved inaccurate, including the news that she was in heaven safe with Jesus. Houdini's mother was Jewish and she barely spoke English, the language the messages had been written in. Houdini became increasingly critical of mediums, which Doyle, found problematic.

A poster from Houdini's tour (campaign) to expose false mediums.

THE ALLURE OF SPIRITUALISM

The 1800s were a time of great change. Huge strides were being made in science, and the Industrial Revolution and related advances in science and technology seemed to promise a better life for all. Yet there was also a frighteningly high infant and child mortality rate with estimates showing 20 per cent of babies died before their first birthday, and up to 25 per cent of children died before the age of five[18]. Poor sanitation, the toxic cloud of pollution pumped out of the new factories that hung over cities, child labour, horrific work conditions and the high rate of industrial accidents, in addition to the many insidious diseases that ran rampant through the big city slums were all contributing factors.

The pall of death sent countless Victorians on a journey to find ways to contact their dearly departed and morbid curiosity fuelled the desire of many to comprehend the mysteries of life, death and the afterlife. This obsession was often characterized by its distinctive blend of scientific progress, spiritual curiosity and a desperation on the part of the grieving to believe in the powers of mystical inanimate objects and spirit mediums.

It's hard to determine which came first. Did the fascination with spiritualism in the Victorian era respond to an emotional need to deal with grief? Or did the Victorians' seemingly perpetual mourning serve as a catalyst for opportunistic charlatans to prey upon the broken hearts of the living? Whatever the answer, spiritualism gained significant momentum in the mid-nineteenth century, appealing to a wide range of individuals across different social classes and promoting the idea that the human spirit survived beyond the death of the body and that it was possible to establish contact with those no longer walking this earthly plane.

Seances where individuals attempted to communicate with the dead became a widespread phenomena during this time. Mediums claimed to bridge the gap between the living and the spirit world, captivating the imaginations of the attendees. Seances, as a central practice of spiritualism, held a particular allure. These gatherings involved a group of people sitting together in a dimly lit room, attempting to contact spirits through various means, such as table turning, automatic writing or direct communication with the dearly departed through the strained vocal cords of a medium. Often women, these spiritualists claimed to possess a unique gift that allowed them to connect with the dead. By 1849, only one year after their first supernatural experience, the Fox sisters were performing before crowds as large as 400 people. As more and more 'evidence' began to pour out of the scientific community that communicating with the dead was a reality, this proved to solidify the public's belief in spiritualism and the authenticity of mediums like the Fox sisters. The sisters were the darlings of the spiritualism world, Gothic icons with a fanbase to match their fame.

This spectacle of mediums summoning spirits captivated the imaginations of Victorians. It became a popular form of entertainment at private

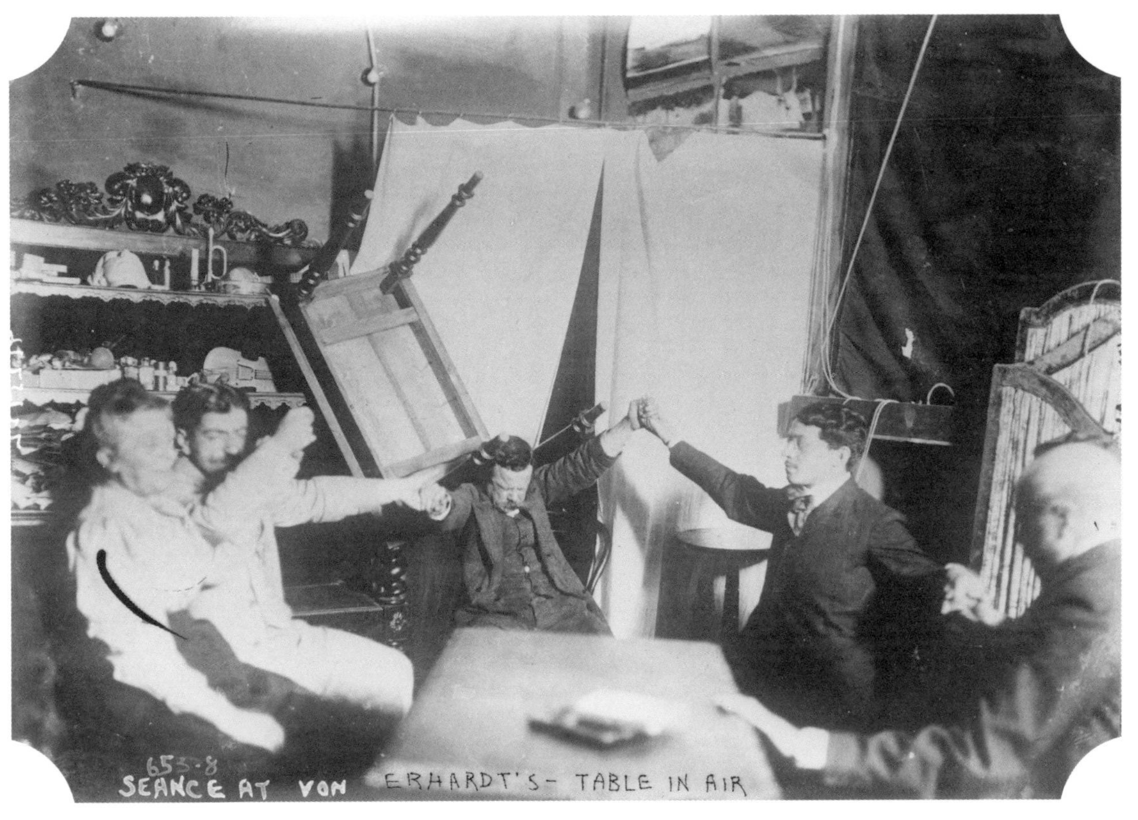

Heavily circulated photos of the violent table levitations and furniture movements at a séance at Baron von Erhardt's Rome studio in 1909.

events. The newly emerging, more moneyed middle class had the financial means to indulge in this growing trend, seances often requiring the payment of a fee to the medium.

Spiritualism, with its emphasis on the afterlife and the moral guidance provided by spirits, also appealed to the Victorian sense of propriety. Many saw it as a way to reinforce and uphold their moral values, especially in the face of societal changes such as the erosion of traditional values, the vices that come with big city life and Darwin's theory of evolution, which challenged the age old religious beliefs brought about by industrialization and urbanization.

A WALK BACK IN TIME

Imagine yourself back in mid to late nineteenth-century London. It's about 9.30 p.m. Greenwich Mean Time, and you've decided to accompany your paramour to an evening of otherworldly entertainment. You find yourself in a dimly lit parlour of a grand mansion, the air is heavy with the scent of incense, which lends an otherworldly, yet exotic atmosphere to the room.

Heavy drapery adorns the windows, shrouding the space in secrecy as the world outside fades into obscurity. A small nondescript table is centre stage in the flickering candlelight, its nicks, scratches and droplets of wax 'battle scars' from previous interactions with the dead. You are one of a group of finely dressed individuals – of course, you would want to look your best when meeting a loved one who has travelled so far to spend a few precious moments with you – who have gathered for an evening of enigmatic revelation, sitting in hushed anticipation around the table, your faces showing both trepidation and curiosity.

As the room settles into an eerie silence, the only sound that persists is the soft crackling of the candles. Everyone seems to be holding their breath, eyes fixed upon the table, hearts beating in harmony, the rhythm of uncertainty. The medium, a woman draped in dark, flowing robes, her face partially obscured, sits at the head of the table, a conduit between the mortal realm and the world of spirits, where your beloved resides.

Suddenly, a whispering voice emerges from the shadows as if summoned by some unseen force. A spectral presence manifested, speaking through the medium's lips. It is shocking, thrilling, a voice not of this world, transcending the boundaries between living and dead. The words spoken are cryptic though, carrying messages seemingly from beyond the veil, conveying secrets and wisdom to many around the room.

As the seance continues, the room comes alive with uncanny phenomena. The table begins to vibrate, its legs lifting from the ground as if possessed by some invisible entity. Wide-eyed and trembling, you cling to your chairs, your disbelief warring with awe mirrored on the faces around you. The medium's hands, seemingly guided by an invisible force, dance above the table, her fingertips grazing its surface as she communicates with the spirits.

Rapping sounds echo through the room, like the distant drumming of ethereal fingers upon the walls. The spirits communicate through these mysterious knocks, answering questions and providing glimpses into the great unknown. Each rap holds a meaning, deciphered for you by this woman who has delved deep into the language of the spirits.

Suddenly, an eerie, ghostly presence materializes before the stunned participants. A pale, translucent figure drifts through the room, barely discernible in the dim light. Someone gasps, most of you can only gaze in astonishment. Has a spirit from the other side crossed the threshold between the worlds? Will it leave an indelible mark on the people present, all witnessed its spectral presence?

Spirit horns, glowing eerily green, held by invisible hands (you find out later those hands were string and thread), emit mournful, otherworldly melodies, filling the room with haunting music. The sorrowful wail of the horns mingles with the whispered voices and rapping sounds, now mysteriously emanating from behind the velvet drapery lining the room. It's a symphony of the supernatural. You are mesmerized. It's like nothing you have seen before.

As the seance draws to a close, you are all left in a state of profound wonder and uncertainty. The dark, candlelit room, heavy with the scent of beeswax candles and incense and the and the enigmatic phenomena you have just witnessed has transported you to a realm beyond the ordinary, where the boundaries between the living and the dead blur and the mysteries of the afterlife beckon. In this Victorian- parlour, you know you have glimpsed the inexplicable. Your belief in the supernatural is forever etched into your soul.

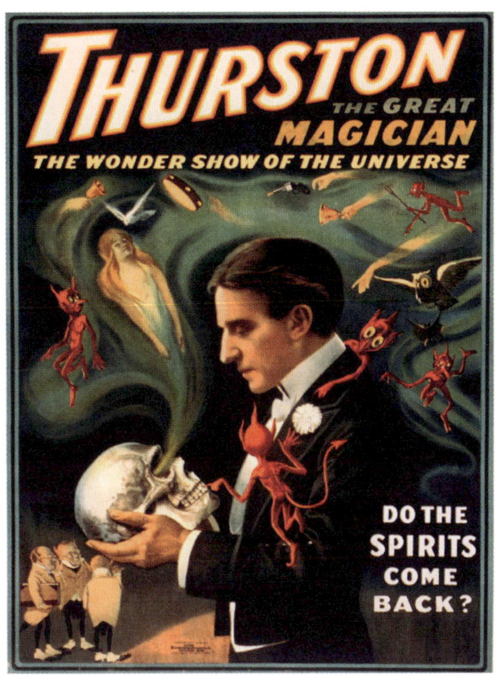

Themes of making contact with the dead became popular in magicians' stage acts.

BACK TO 'REALITY'

Let's blow out the candles, turn the electric lights back on and bring you back to the present day – at least physically – because there is more to explain about what may have been present at that seance.

Every year, there appeared to be a keeping-up-with-the-Jones mentality emerging among the spiritualists. To top one another and make their hosted experience more exciting and convincing, a multitude of paranormal paraphernalia were developed and incorporated into each unique experience.

Before the ever-popular Ouija board became the default spiritual conduit, there was the planchette, a simple device with spotty paranormal reception. Planchette translates from French as 'the little plank'. It's a small triangular or heart-shaped board supported on casters at two points and a vertical pencil at a third.

The Ouija board, also known as a spirit board

A stereoscopic slide entitled 'The Haunted Lane' illustrates that even a country lane could be haunted!

or talking board, gained popularity during this period, participants at a seance placing their fingers on a planchette, a small heart-shaped pointer, and asking questions of the spirits, either via a medium or directly. They believed spirits would guide the planchette to spell out answers on the board. Automatic writing such as that experienced by Houdini during the 1922 seance in Atlantic City.

Other things that spiritualists might experience while trying to communicate with the dead included table-turning or table-tipping. Table-turning involved participants sitting around a table and placing their hands on it. They believed that the spirits would move the table, tipping it or making it spin to provide answers to questions or convey messages.

A spirit cabinet was a piece of furniture used by mediums during seances. The medium would enter the cabinet and various objects inside it would move, levitate or produce mysterious sounds, supposedly under the influence of spirits.

Victorian-era spiritualists also experimented with photography to capture images of spirits or ghostly apparitions. Some famous photographs, like the previously mentioned Cottingley Fairies' photographs, were later revealed as hoaxes, but they captured the public's imagination at the time, enthralling supporters like Doyle.

Spiritualism, however, was also met with criticism and scepticism. While many flocked to mediums and dabbled with Ouija boards, debates also raged over the authenticity of such practices and of the people who professed to be able to communicate with the spirits of the dead.

Eva-Carriere summons a glowing ghostly aura to the astonishment of an elderly client.

SPIRIT PHOTOGRAPHY

A surprisingly blank stare from a pair of mediums, especially when a large plume of ectoplasm emanates from their partner's head.

Two popular types of photography made their way into the spiritualist world. These new-fangled camera inventions were the only apparatus that could seemingly capture the presence of supernatural beings invisible to the human eye.

A notable figure in the history of spirit photography was Boston-based William H. Mumler, who claimed to have captured the spirits of the deceased in his portraits. In 1861, Mumler produced a photograph of himself with a ghostly figure standing beside him, which he believed to be the spirit of a deceased friend. While Mumler's work was initially met with suspicion and accusations of fraud, it also gained a substantial following and influenced the popularity of spirit photography during the Victorian era.

William Mumler created his spirit photographs using a technique involving double exposure. He first took a portrait or background image, then re-exposed the same photographic plate with the living subject, causing faint ghostly figures to appear alongside the living – convincing many that they were seeing actual spirits. While popular, not everyone believed in Mumler's abilities and in 1874, he was tried for fraudulently creating spirit photographs. Surprisingly, he was acquitted, and his work continued to gain support.

Spirit photography peaked in popularity in the late nineteenth century, with countless other photographers attempting to capture evidence of the afterlife. William Hope, known for his ghostly double-exposure photographs, was the Mumler of England. Many devotees celebrated his work as genuine evidence of the spirit world, although critics argued that it was merely the result of photographic manipulation.

Players in the spiritualist world were always looking to up their game. That philosophy was applied to spirit photography in one of the most peculiar aspects, manifesting evidence of communicating with the dead. This would come in portraying mediums seemingly producing 'plasma' from various orifices, often depicted as ectoplasmic emanations. This phenomenon has been central to some of the most controversial and sensational spirit photographs ever taken. Ectoplasm is described as a viscous, otherworldly substance that emerges from the medium's nose, mouth or other bodily openings, including their genitalia, during a seance. It is believed to be the materialization of spirits or energy from the spirit world.

One of the most famous practitioners of ectoplasmic spirit photography was French medium Eva Carrière. In the early twentieth century, Carrière worked with renowned psychical researcher Albert von Schrenck-Notzing and produced a series of images featuring her producing ectoplasm from her mouth. These photographs generated both immense interest and controversy. Sceptics argued that the ectoplasm was nothing more than cloth or paper soaked in chemicals expelled by the medium. Despite extensive investigations, the authenticity of these images remains a subject of debate to this day.

Regardless of belief or scepticism, the fascination with the proof of an afterlife and the desire to connect with departed loved ones were defining features of the Victorian era's interest in spiritualism and the lengths they would go to contact their departed loved ones. ❀

A Mumler photo of Mrs. Lincoln where Mumler captured a deceased Abraham lovingly resting his hands on the shoulders of his wife, Mary Todd Lincoln.

CHAPTER VII

The DARK ARTS

A DANCE WITH DEATH IN LITERATURE AND CULTURE

EDGAR ALLEN POE AND BEYOND

The Victorian era saw the creation of some of the most enduring works of English literature, which often grappled with the themes of mortality, dying and the macabre. Perhaps no author is more of a poster boy for this era than Edgar Allan Poe.

Poe spent a few years as a child in England but moved to the States in 1820, aged 11. He never returned to Britain, dying in 1849, some twelve years before Prince Albert, whose demise was the catalyst for the symbolic miasma of death that would seep into every crevice of the Western world, as discussed earlier in this book. Despite much of Poe's work predating the Victorian era, his literary corpus resonated with readers of this time and his writings grew in popularity and influence as the century waned.

This was an age, as we have seen, characterized by strict social mores, a burgeoning middle class, significant scientific progress, a high mortality rate and a deep fascination with the macabre, the supernatural and the boundaries of human experience. The Industrial Revolution was transforming landscapes and lives yet it also engendered a sense of dislocation and existential dread among Victorians, themes that were echoed in much of Poe's work.

Classic portrait of Edgar Allan Poe (1809-1849). Photographer and date unknown.

Some of his most famous storylines revolved around madness and death, themes which resonated with Victorian readers. His focus on inner turmoil and decay was exemplified in such tales as the 1839 'The Fall of the House of Usher'. Here a man visits a childhood friend, Roderick Usher, suffering from physical and mental illness, in a decaying mansion. Roderick's twin sister, Madeline, dies and is entombed and the mansion collapses into the lake, symbolizing the family Ushers' doom and the merging of their fate with the house. Similarly, his 1843 'The Tell-Tale Heart' is a story told by an unnamed narrator who becomes obsessed with an old man's 'vulture-like' eye and, driven by madness, he murders him. However, the narrator's guilt overwhelms him and he imagines hearing the relentless beating of the dead man's heart, leading him to confess the crime.

Poe's 'The Premature Burial', published in 1844 in *The Philadelphia Dollar Newspaper*, has its main character fearing the possibility of being buried alive. This was not only a concern of the fictional unnamed narrator of the story but also a fear that gripped Poe and many other people of his time. More than a few cases of premature burials – some fabricated to sell newspapers, but others authentic, pop up in periodicals. This fear, as previously discussed, can be seen in the intricacies of Victorian burial sites, where bells and air tubes were not uncommon devices. Poe's work mirrored the early Victorians' anxieties about morality, sanity, death and the dark undercurrents of the human psyche.

Academics have cited Poe's meticulous attention to atmosphere and setting connected with the Gothic Revival architectural trends of the time. Literary figures such as the poet Charles Baudelaire, best known for his poem '*Les Fleurs du mal*' (1857; 'The Flowers of Evil'), who translated Poe's work into French, and Sir Arthur Conan Doyle, of Sherlock Holmes' fame, promoted his work in the UK, and gave Poe international success.

One of the most notable examples of Victorian literature influenced by the era's obsession with death is Charles Dickens's *A Christmas Carol* (1843). While ultimately a tale of redemption, this novella is steeped in the themes of mortality and the supernatural. The protagonist, Ebenezer Scrooge, is confronted by the ghosts of his past, present and future, forcing him to confront his mortality and the consequences of his actions. Dickens uses these spectral visitations to explore the idea of death as a catalyst for moral awakening and change.

Thomas Hardy is another significant figure in Victorian literature, whose novels often depict the harsh realities of life and the inevitability of death. He challenged societal mores with characters dealing with the hardships of working-class people. In *Tess of the d'Urbervilles* (1891), Hardy portrays the tragic fate of his eponymous character, a woman doomed by the social and moral constraints of her time. The novel's bleak outlook on life and death highlights the deterministic view of existence prevalent at the time.

Two classics written at the height of the Victorian era were Emily Brontë's 1847 *Wuthering Heights* and Bram Stoker's 1897 *Drácula*. *Wuthering Heights* is renowned for its intricate narrative that masterfully intertwines Gothic elements within its tragic romance. The novel is set against the bleak and brooding backdrop of the Yorkshire moors, a setting that perfectly complements the dark themes and moody atmosphere that pervade the story.

An 1870 Sol Eytinge, Jr. engraving from *A Christmas Carol* by Charles Dickens.

Despite much of Poe's work predating the Victorian era, his literary corpus resonated with readers of this time .

The 1939 version of *Wuthering Heights* starring David Niven and directed by William Wyler.

The Gothic overtones are vividly embodied in the foreboding Wuthering Heights, a haunted house filled with echoes of past traumas and ghostly presences. The characters are deeply flawed and tortured, often driven by passions that border on the supernatural. Heathcliff, the enigmatic and predominantly malevolent protagonist, personifies an antihero as characterized by his deep drive for revenge and seemingly otherworldly endurance and will. Although the book ends with a glimmer of hope, two of the main characters seem fated to wander the moors together in death.

Brontë uses supernatural elements in her novel, such as ghostly apparitions and premonitions, to heighten the sense of mystery and terror, crafting a narrative that explores the darker side of human emotions and delves into the paranormal.

Although, writing on the cusp of the Victorian and Edwardian eras, Edith Wharton drew from the dark undercurrents of her predecessors to craft a literary legacy steeped in haunting atmospheres and biting social critique. Her storytelling inherited the era's penchant for exploring the grim and shadowed corners of human existence, yet she injected a distinctly modern edge, exposing the psychological turmoil simmering beneath the surface of her characters.

In novels like *Ethan Frome* and short stories such as "Afterward," Wharton channeled the Victorian era's preoccupation with death, decay, and the supernatural into settings that blurred the line between the haunted and the merely desolate. She masterfully wove themes of isolation, unfulfilled desires, and the spectral presence of guilt, creating narratives where the past relentlessly lingers, much like a restless ghost.

FRANKENSTEIN VS DRÁCULA

Any modern-day conversation regarding literature's most renowned horror classics undoubtedly would include Mary Shelley's *Frankenstein* and Bram Stoker's *Drácula*. Written almost 80 years apart, 1818 and 1897, respectively, these two works were staples of Victorian society's must-reads. However, both were not immune to ethical criticism.

Mary Shelley's *Frankenstein* or *The Modern Prometheus* and Bram Stoker's *Drácula* are seminal works in the Gothic horror genre and share striking similarities in their themes and the societal reactions they provoked. Both delve into the macabre and explore the boundaries of human experience, particularly focusing on the themes of life, death and the unnatural. *Frankenstein* tells the story of Victor Frankenstein, a scientist who defies the natural order by creating life from death. His monstrous creation, often mistakenly referred to as Frankenstein, symbolizes the hubris of humanity and the dire consequences of playing God. Shelley's novel is deeply rooted in

Frankenstein, the 1931 Universal film with Boris Karloff and Marilyn Harris.

Bram Stoker by W. & D. Downey.
A photogravure (c.1906).

the Romantic era's preoccupations with nature, individualism and the sublime, but it also foreshadows Victorian concerns about scientific progress and moral responsibility. Dr Frankenstein's transgression of natural boundaries and the resulting horror reflect the anxieties of a society grappling with rapid technological and scientific advancements.

Drácula encapsulates the fears and anxieties of the late Victorian era, when the British Empire was at its zenith but also experiencing profound social and cultural shifts. Stoker's novel introduces Count Dracula, an ancient vampire who travels from Transylvania to England to spread his curse.

The character of Drácula embodies the fear of the unknown and the foreign, reflecting Victorian anxieties about immigration, disease and the erosion of traditional values. The vampire's immortality and his predation on the living highlight a morbid fascination with death and the undead, themes that were particularly resonant in a society obsessed with funerary practices and the afterlife.

Despite their different historical contexts, *Frankenstein* and *Drácula* captivated the Victorian imagination. Notoriously preoccupied with death, this cultural backdrop provided fertile ground for the success of both novels. However, their reception revealed the era's ambivalence towards such macabre themes. On the one hand, the stories fed into a collective fascination with the Gothic and the grotesque; on the other, they also provoked discomfort and moral outrage.

Victorian readers and critics were intellectually stimulated by Shelley's and Stoker's works and emotionally moved. *Frankenstein* was seen as a cautionary tale about the dangers of unchecked scientific ambition and the moral responsibilities of creators. The novel's depiction of a monstrous being rejected by society and its tragic consequences resonated with contemporary concerns about social alienation and the limits of human knowledge. Similarly, *Drácula* was interpreted as reflecting societal fears about degeneration and the loss of moral and physical purity. The novel's erotic undertones and portrayal of the vampire's violation of societal norms challenged Victorian propriety, leading to its mixed emotional reception.

Despite the controversy, the enduring popularity of *Frankenstein* and *Drácula* is not just a testament to their ability to tap into the deepest fears and fascinations of their time but also serves as a reminder of their timeless relevance. They continue to reflect the anxieties of an era obsessed with mortality and the boundaries of human experience, resonating with readers across generations and cultures.

DOOM AND GLOOM IN IAMBIC PENTAMETER

Throughout the ages, poetry's popularity has experienced highs and lows. In the mid-1800s–early 1900s, poetry flourished as a beloved form of literature, giving rise to some of the most famous and enduring works, many known for their macabre themes.

Is it fair to accuse Robert Louis Stevenson, Alfred Tennyson, Oscar Wilde and many other writers of falling victim to the era's preoccupation with death and sorrow? Did it impact on their psyches to the point where they were driven to produce novels and poetry devoted to dying and grief? The answer is a resounding 'no'. This outpouring of pain came from life experience in an era rife with pain and suffering, and their work proved to be an elixir that intoxicated the morose masses of the mid-1800s to the early 1900s.

Tennyson's 'In Memoriam A.H.H.' (1850), a poignant exploration of grief and loss, was written in memory of his close friend Arthur Hallam, a Cambridge alumnus who died of a cerebral hemorrhage. Wilde's 'The Ballad of Reading Gaol' (1898) is a moving and reflective poem that dives into the bleak reality of prison life and the inevitability of death. Written during Wilde's two-year imprisonment for gross indecency (homosexuality was illegal at the time), the poem chronicles the execution of a fellow inmate, juxtaposing the brutality of the act with meditations on human suffering and the inescapable nature of mortality.

Based on the voluminous amount of gloomy work he produced, Edgar Allan Poe could have grown up in Disneyland and he would still have found it virtually impossible to pen anything but morbid tales and frighteningly depressing

Portrait of the playwright and novelist Oscar Wilde (1854-1900) by Napoleon Sarony (c.1882).

poetry. Poe's 'The Raven' (1845), a quintessential Gothic poem, exemplifies the period's obsession with death and the supernatural. The poem's narrator, grieving the loss of his beloved Lenore, is visited by a mysterious raven that repeatedly utters the word 'Nevermore'. This refrain becomes a haunting reminder of the permanence of death and the futility of seeking solace in the afterlife. Poe's masterful use of rhythm and rhyme, combined with dark, eerie imagery, creates an atmosphere of despair and inevitability. As a symbol of death and the unknown, the raven taps into the Victorian fascination with mourning, the supernatural and the psychological effects of loss and grief. The poem's exploration of madness, sorrow and the search for meaning in the face of death resonated with the masses of the time.

Christina Rossetti's 'Goblin Market' (1862) takes a slightly more 'colourful' approach to the same topics that Poe, Tennyson and Wilde explore. However, it is far from 'macabre-lite'. While seemingly a fairy tale, this poem is rife with dark undertones of temptation, sin and redemption. The goblins, symbolizing the allure of sin, prey upon the innocence of two young girls, leading to a devastating outcome. The poem thus explores the boundary between life and death, the consequences of succumbing to temptation and the implications for one's morality and the afterlife, all very Victorian themes.

Although there were some bright spots through the period, much of Victorian literature is a poignant mirror of society, vividly reflecting humanity's deep-seated fears and perpetual societal woes with eloquent, enduring resonance.

BETTER OFF DEAD?

Another area popular with Victorian 'entertainment' were carnival-based shows. While such freak shows can trace their origins to earlier centuries, they reached their zenith during the nineteenth century, audiences flocking to see these travelling cabinets of human curiosities. They capitalized on the Victorian fascination with science, anatomy and the boundaries of human potential and interest in perfection and deformity. Sometimes, the 'exhibits' were seen as a comment on how close one could come to death without really being dead. At other times, audiences would come to gawk at dead and living medical oddities. The dead displayed in oversized 'gas' jars filled with alcohol or formaldehyde, usually contained a deformed fetus or infant. Living medical oddities could be found sitting on a dimly lit stage, behind bars or in a dark tent naked or nearly naked so the audience could marvel at every inch of their biological misfortune.

These exhibitions often exploited marginalized people, many of whom had few options for making a living in 'normal' society.

The proprietors of these shows, men like P.T. Barnum, capitalized on the public's fascination with 'freaks', often under the guise of scientific inquiry. Performers, including those with dwarfism, conjoined twins, and individuals with conditions like albinism or hypertrichosis

Portrait photo (c.1860) of the tiny stars of P T Barnum's 19th century shows standing alongside a 'giant'.

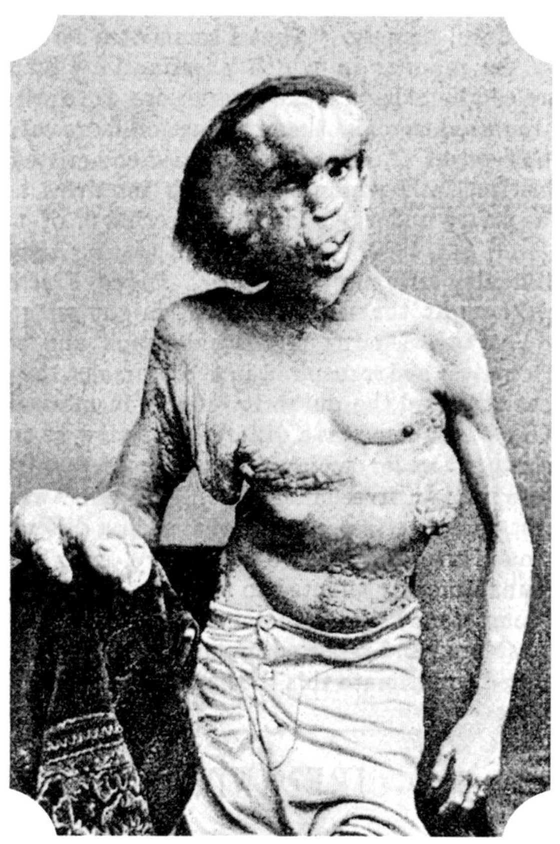

A formal portrait of Joseph Carey Merrick, known as the 'Elephant Man' c.1888.

(excessive hair growth), were treated as spectacles rather than human beings.

Due to economic desperation, many of these individuals were coerced or forced into performing, sometimes by their own families. They had virtually no control over their working conditions, how much they were paid or how they were portayed in the advertisements -- always with their uniqueness exaggerated or fabricated to draw larger crowds, further dehumanizing them.

While some performers were able to achieve relative financial independence through their participation, they were nonetheless subjected to exploitation and humiliation. Victorian freak shows highlight the era's darker tendencies towards the commodification of human bodies, especially those considered 'abnormal'.

Joseph Merrick, better known to modern audiences as 'The Elephant Man', was born in Leicester, in the East Midlands, in 1862. From an early age, Merrick developed severe physical deformities due to a congenital disorder, now believed to be either Proteus syndrome [19] or neurofibromatosis [20]. His condition caused large, tumorous growths on his skin, an enlarged head and distorted limbs. These abnormalities made life incredibly difficult for him, both physically and socially.

At the age of 12, following the death of his mother, Merrick was sent to a workhouse, a harsh institution for the poor. Eventually, Merrick became part of a travelling freak show, where he was exhibited under the stage name 'The Elephant Man'. This brought him to London, where he came to the attention of Dr Frederick Treves, a surgeon at the London Hospital. Treves took an interest in Merrick's case, ultimately rescuing him from exploitation and offering him a permanent home in the hospital.

Despite his outward appearance, Merrick was known for his gentle and intelligent nature. He enjoyed reading, writing poetry and building intricate models, one of which was a detailed cardboard model of St Philip's Church, which still exists and can be seen at the Royal London Hospital Museum in Whitechapel, London. Merrick formed friendships with several upper-class Londoners, who, under Treves's guidance, visited him at the hospital, offering him a taste of social acceptance.

Joseph Merrick died at the age of 27 in 1890. His death was likely accidental; it is believed that in an attempt to sleep lying down – something he could not usually do due to the size of his head – he suffocated. Merrick's skeleton was preserved for medical study and kept at the Royal London Hospital Museum. His story is immortalized in a 1980 film, starring John Hurt as Merrick.

LIGHTS. CAMERA. DEATH.

Although filmmaking was in its infancy, the Victorians' fascination with death significantly influenced the art form, particularly in the creation of early horror films by pioneers like the Lumière Brothers and Georges Méliès.

The Lumière brothers, Auguste and Louis, were French inventors and pioneers in early cinema. Born in the 1860s, they worked in their family's photographic business. They are credited with developing the groundbreaking Cinématographe, a camera-projector hybrid that revolutionized motion pictures. In 1895, they held the first public screening of projected films in Paris, marking the birth of cinema as a mass entertainment medium. Their short films, such as *Arrival of a Train at La Ciotat*, fascinated audiences.

While they are best known for their documentary-style films, they also ventured into horror. Their 1897 short film *Le Squelette Joyeux* (The Merry Skeleton) exemplifies their engagement with death-related themes. In this film, a skeleton performs a macabre dance, delighting and unsettling audiences. The film's playful yet unsettling tone reflects the era's response to death, blending fear with a sense of curiosity and wonder.

Méliès, a contemporary of the Lumière Brothers, took a more explicit and innovative approach to horror. A magician turned filmmaker, he is renowned for his groundbreaking use of special effects and narrative storytelling in cinema. Méliès' *Le Manoir du Diable* (1896; The Haunted Castle) is often regarded as the first horror film.

The magically suspended head in Georges Méliès' stage illusion *La Source Enchantée* in Paris, 1892.

It features a series of supernatural occurrences, including ghosts, skeletons and a demonic bat, all conjured through Méliès' ingenious use of stop-motion effects and theatrical tricks.

These early horror films, with their ability to evoke fear, curiosity and wonder, laid the foundation for the genre and marked a significant milestone in the development of cinema. It would be more than two decades before the world would see and hear the first movie with sound. Enjoying music was still relegated to the theatre and the opera house.

Guionie as Violetta in Verdi's opera *La Traviata* at the Theatre National del' Opera Comique, Paris, c.1904.

FROM ARIAS TO FUNERAL DIRGES

Giuseppe Verdi's opera *La Traviata*, premiering in 1853, intertwines the tragic story of love and death through the lens of tuberculosis. The opera, based on Alexandre Dumas fils' play *La Dame aux Camélias*, centres on Violetta Valéry, a Parisian courtesan suffering from the disease. Her illness is not merely a personal affliction but also a pivotal plot device that impacts her relationships and societal standing.

The opera emphasizes the notions of consumption being associated with beauty, artistic sensitivity and tragic youth. This romanticization of tuberculosis is evident in Violetta's character, whose ethereal beauty and tragic fate are accentuated by her illness. Verdi's composition of *La Traviata* delicately balances the harsh realities of the disease with the societal perceptions of the time. The music poignantly conveys Violetta's internal struggle and physical deterioration, using her coughing fits and weakening voice to heighten the drama and elicit sympathy. Verdi's nuanced portrayal of the disease – both as a literal sickness and a symbolic representation of societal decay – critically engages with Victorian morbidity, reflecting on the broader implications of illness and death in society.

Victorian music also echoed themes of death and grief, often in the form of funeral marches and dirges. A notable example is the *Funeral March*, composed by Frederic Chopin, which became highly popular in Victorian society for its solemn and reflective mood. Additionally, the period saw the creation of other musical works that explored themes of the supernatural and the afterlife, mirroring the era's obsession with spiritualism and communication with the dead.

There is no denying that masterpieces in so many art forms were created during the Victorian era. However, no aspect of the arts was safe from the blanket of doom draped over the Western world, resulting in a body of work that beautifully expresses the pain of human suffering. ❀

The music poignantly conveys Violetta's internal struggle and physical deterioration, using her coughing fits and weakening voice to heighten the drama and elicit sympathy.

CHAPTER VIII

MEMENTO MORI

KEEPSAKES OF THE DEAD

FROM GILGAMISH TO JESUS CHRIST

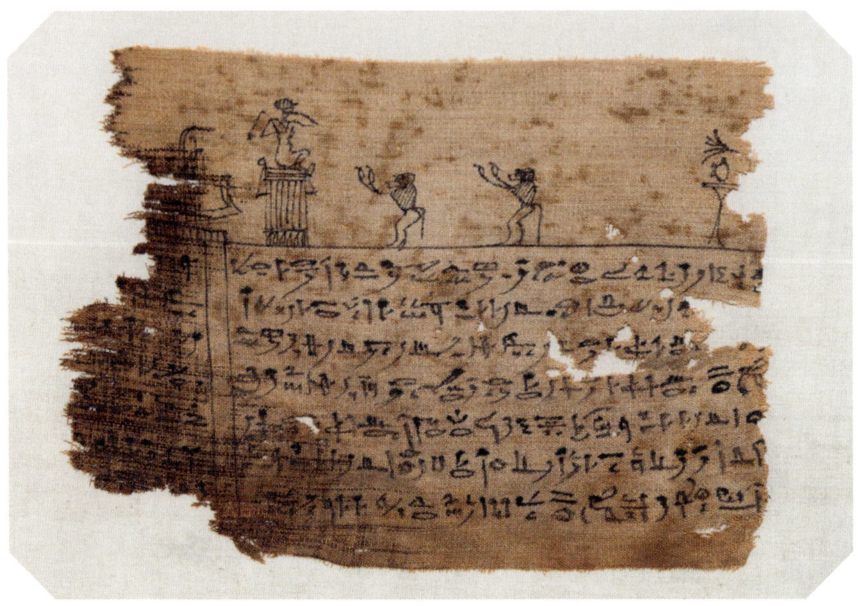

Known collectively as the *Book of the Dead*, these Egyptian ritual spells were inscribed on funerary objects, including papyrus scrolls and linen mummy wrappings.

The fascination with mortality was not a new phenomenon ushered in with the Victorian era. From the dawn of human civilization, the concepts of death and the impermanence of life have been a source of intrigue and terror. This duality of fascination and fear has profoundly influenced religion, philosophy, art and culture throughout history. If we go as far back as Mesopotamia, founded around 4,000 BC, the *Epic of Gilgamesh* offers one of the earliest literary explorations of death and immortality. The story follows Gilgamesh, a king who embarks on a quest to find eternal life after the death of his friend Enkidu. Ultimately, Gilgamesh learns that immortality is reserved for the gods and that humans must find meaning in their finite lives.

Although their belief on who gets a ticket to the afterlife and who doesn't, differed from the Mesopotamians, the ancient Egyptians shared the same deep preoccupation with death and the afterlife. They left behind thousands of physical manifestations of this obsession. Their elaborate burial practices and monumental tombs, such as the pyramids, reflect a belief in an eternal life beyond death. The Egyptian *Book of the Dead* is a series of ancient ritual spells, instructions and incantations to help the deceased find their way to the afterlife and unite with the sun god, Re, and the netherworld god, Osiris. As the controversial Egyptologist Zahi Hawass notes, 'For the ancient Egyptians, death was not an end but a transition to another plane of existence.' Hawass has been accused of controlling access to digs and silencing opposing voices, illegal trafficking of Egyptian antiquities and attributing all major discoveries to Egyptians rather than foreign influences. Despite this, his contributions to understanding ancient Egypt's views on death and the afterlife are widely acknowledged

The Greeks, led by philosophers like Epicurus, Socrates and Plato, took a very different approach to the Egyptians. Instead of spending vast amounts of time, energy and money on the physically deceased, they instead intellectualized what a person should do while alive – primarily live a life that allows one to be 'ready' for one's inevitable death. The philosopher Socrates famously discussed death in Plato's *Phaedo*, where he asserts, 'The one aim of those who practise philosophy in the proper manner is to practise for dying and death.'

Christianity introduced a transformative perspective on death and the afterlife. The teachings of Jesus Christ emphasized eternal life through faith and resurrection, offering a hopeful alternative to the fear of death. Unfortunately, those hopeful views within Christianity took a gut punch during the medieval period, where death was a constant presence due to plagues and high infant mortality rates, thus putting the presence of God under scrutiny. The Black Death, the plague that ravaged Europe in the fourteenth century, brought death to the forefront of collective consciousness.

The concept of 'memento mori', or 'remember that you will die', became a common theme in art and literature. The medieval Christians who managed to hold true to their faith were encouraged to live piously in preparation for the afterlife, as illustrated by the words of Thomas à Kempis, a German-Dutch Catholic cleric of the late medieval period, in *The Imitation of Christ*: 'Every action of yours, every thought, should be those of one who expects to die before the day is out.'

THE DANSE MACABRE

Europe in the 1300s and 1400s had primitive medical care, two significant plagues and a fair share of bloody wars, including part of the Hundred Years' War (1337–1453) and the Wars of the Roses (1455–87), rendering the time oh too familiar with the nondiscriminatory scythe of the Grim Reaper. One of the most striking artistic representations of medieval attitudes towards death is the 'Danse Macabre' or 'Dance of Death'. This allegorical concept depicted death as a skeleton leading people of all social classes to their graves, emphasizing the inevitability

'Dance of Death' (aka Danse Macabre) from *Liber Chronicarum*, Hartmann Schedel, published in 1493.

and universality of death. The Dance of Death served as a reminder that death spares no one, regardless of wealth or status. It reflected the era's grim reality and a potential call to repentance and humility.

The earliest known use of the term 'memento mori' in popular culture was in the late 1500s. Playwright William Shakespeare brought it to the attention of many in his play *Henry IV*: 'I make as good use of it as many a man doth of a Death's-head or a memento more[21]. Yet it is not the first mention of the phrase. In fact, the history of 'memento mori' (commonly misspelled as *momento* mori) is shrouded in controversy, with scores of scholars attributing the origin to various now extinct cultures, some ancient. The earliest record of 'memento mori' is alleged to have been recounted as a chorus by a Black or Syrian slave of a Roman general.

'Memento mori' is part of a three-sentence phrase: '*Respice post te. Hominem te esse memento. Memento mori!*' That is, 'Look behind. Remember, thou art mortal. Remember, you must die!'

After a significant military victory, triumphant generals were paraded through their home city to the roaring adoration of the masses. These grand processions, sometimes lasting an entire day, featured the military leader standing in a chariot drawn by four horses. This was the pinnacle of honour. The general was idolized and viewed as divine by his troops and the public. But behind the worshipped general, standing in the same chariot, was a slave whose sole duty during the entire procession was to whisper, '*Respice post te. Hominem te esse memento. Memento mori!*' This slave served to remind the victor, even at the peak of glory, that the god-like adoration would end, but the truth of his mortality would remain.

Although morbid, these axioms had a common theme of availing people to appreciate life, enjoy the here and now and be a better human being while here on this earth.

THE 'MODERN' CONTEXT

The concept of memento mori gained renewed prominence during the Victorian period. This resurgence can be attributed to several interrelated factors, including religious beliefs, high mortality rates and evolving cultural practices surrounding death and mourning. Victorians were acutely aware of the transient nature of life, a perspective that was reinforced by the pervasive presence of death in their daily lives. Tuberculosis, cholera and typhus were rampant, claiming lives indiscriminately and often prematurely. Child mortality was exceptionally high and many families experienced the heart-wrenching loss of young children. In this context, memento mori keepsakes served as personal and poignant reminders of loved ones lost and the inevitability of death.

Religious beliefs played a significant role in the popularity of memento mori during the Victorian era. Christianity, particularly in its Protestant form, was the dominant faith in Britain and the United States, and it emphasized the importance of living a virtuous life in preparation for the afterlife. Memento mori artifacts were not merely morbid tokens but were intended to encourage moral reflection and spiritual readiness. By contemplating mortality, individuals were reminded of the fleeting nature of earthly existence and the necessity of living by Christian virtues to attain salvation. These keepsakes often featured religious symbols such as crosses, angels, and biblical inscriptions, reinforcing their spiritual purpose.

Moreover, the Victorian fascination with death and memento mori can be understood in the context of the era's artistic and aesthetic sensibilities. The period was marked by a romanticization of death, reflected in literature, art, and architecture. Gothic Revival architecture was particularly popular with its sombre and macabre elements. Memento mori keepsakes, with their skilled craftsmanship and symbolic designs, were extensions of this aesthetic. They were cherished for their personal significance and as works of art that encapsulated the Victorian preoccupation with beauty, decay and the passage of time.

The technological advancements of the Industrial Revolution also contributed to the proliferation of remembrance items. Improved manufacturing techniques and the rise of consumer culture made these keepsakes affordable and, therefore, more accessible to a broader segment of society. In particular, photography revolutionized how people commemorated their deceased loved ones. Post-mortem photography became common, in which the recently deceased were photographed as if still alive. These photographs were often incorporated into lockets or framed as keepsakes, providing a lasting visual memory of the departed.

LOCKETS OF LOST LOVES

The mourning ring often featured black enamel or jet, a fossilized wood used extensively in Victorian mourning pieces. The band of the ring was sometimes inscribed with the deceased's name, age, and date of death, transforming it into a wearable epitaph. Some rings contained compartments for holding a lock of the deceased's hair, meticulously woven into intricate patterns and set under glass.

Lockets were another prevalent form of mourning jewellery. These small, pendant-like pieces could be worn close to the heart, symbolizing the enduring emotional bond between the living and the dead. Victorian lockets often contained miniature illustrated portraits or photographs of the deceased, capturing their likeness in a moment of life. More intimately, like the rings, they also housed locks of hair woven into shapes or complex designs. In America, during the Civil War, mothers, wives, and sweethearts would clip a lock of a soldier's hair before he left. In the unfortunate event he never returned, that hair would be woven into a piece of mourning jewellery.

These lockets were sometimes adorned with pearls, symbolizing tears, and could be highly ornate, while others were starkly simple. It was said that these designs were reflective of personal taste and the extent of the mourner's grief. However, it seems unfair to generalize a simplistically styled ring to denote the mourner's lack of grief and more a reflection of their financial limitations.

Brooches, too, played a significant role in mourning attire. Again, jet was a common material, its deep black colour embodying the sombreness of mourning. Some brooches were crafted in the shape of anchors, symbolizing hope, or urns, representing the soul's passage to the afterlife. Using seed pearls in brooches, representing tears, added an additional layer of meaning. Hairwork brooches, similar to rings and lockets, often contained woven hair of the deceased. These pieces could be quite elaborate, showcasing the Victorian era's mastery of hair art.

The mourning bracelet again, used the hair of the deceased and these bracelets were often adorned with gold or silver clasps. Some featured miniature lockets or medallions holding photographs or tiny portraits. Weaving the hair of a loved one into a bracelet was both a craft and a ritual, allowing the mourner to engage in a meditative process of remembrance. They were worn as daily reminders of loss, intertwining grief with the physical form.

Earrings, although less common, were also a part of mourning jewellery. Jet was the predominant material, often carved into teardrop shapes or other sombre designs. The choice of earrings was typically more restrained, reflecting the mourning period's strict etiquette and the subdued nature of grief.

As delicate and sombre pieces, mourning jewellery served as a poignant expression of grief and a memento of lost loved ones with a blending of artistry that carried deep personal significance.

A hand-painted pin on an enamel base. Incredibly detailed, the 'Rest In Hope' is pristine, tiny pearls are incorporated into the piece, c.1790.

IT IS WITH A HEAVY HEART . . .

Mourning stationery and announcements were vital in grief rituals, as formal notifications of loss and personal expressions of sorrow. These pieces were meticulously designed to reflect the era's strict mourning customs, symbolic of the mourner's grief and respect for the deceased.

A popular example of mourning stationery was the mourning letterhead. These sheets of paper were typically black, the border's width reflecting how close the sender was to the deceased. For instance, a widowed spouse might use stationery with a broad black border, while a more distant relative a narrower one. The paper was often high-quality, usually off-white or grey, and sometimes adorned with discreet black embellishments such as crosses, urns or weeping willows. The mourning letterhead ensured that every correspondence conveyed the appropriate tone of solemnity.

Accompanying the mourning letterhead were black-edged envelopes. Like the letterhead, these envelopes had black borders and sometimes featured a small, tasteful symbol of mourning on the back flap. The address would be written in dark ink, often with a flourish that mirrored the ornate penmanship of the era. Sending and receiving such an envelope was an unmistakable sign of bereavement, and the very sight of it in the mail would prepare the recipient for the sorrowful news contained within.

Mourning cards were another essential element of Victorian mourning stationery. These small cards were used to announce a death or to thank individuals for their condolences and support. They were typically printed on heavy, high-quality card stock, bordered in black, and often featured an emblem of mourning, such as an angel, an urn or a wreath. The text was usually printed in black or dark grey ink, with an elegant, flowing script that added a touch of grace to 'soften' the sombre message. Mourning cards were sent to family, friends and acquaintances, ensuring that the news of the loss was communicated with the appropriate decorum.

Visiting cards, or calling cards, were also adapted for mourning. These were sometimes simple and, at other times, ornate personal cards that were sent or dropped off at a relative's or friend's home during periods of mourning. They often included a brief, printed message announcing a death and indicating the mourner's temporary seclusion due to their grief.

Mourning remembrance cabinet cards were a staple among the bereaving well-to-do. These were formal announcements and remembrance pieces printed on thick black cardboard with rounded corners, commonly with accents in gold foil or metallic ink. In addition to the details of the deceased, such as the name, date of death and age, they also included an appropriate religious passage and, sometimes, a small, tasteful illustration or motif related to mourning would be included, such as a dove, a cross or a draped urn, adding a visual element to the solemn text.

Memorial books or mourning albums were

another poignant example of mourning stationery. These books were used to collect and preserve letters of condolence, funeral notices and other mementos related to the deceased. They were bound in black or dark-coloured leather, with the deceased's name or initials embossed on the cover. Inside, pages were made of heavy, high-quality paper, sometimes with black borders or printed decorations. These albums served as cherished keepsakes, allowing mourners to revisit the expressions of sympathy and remembrance from friends and family.

M

Le Vicomte de Kerret, Madame de la Sablière, la Vicomtesse
du Bouëxic de la Driennays, le
Signières, le Baron et la Baronn
de la Sablière, Mademoiselle
Hersart du Buron, le Vicom
la Driennays, Mademoiselle
Monsieur Philippe de Bourb
de Bourbon, Monsieur Antoin
Madeleine Séguier, Monsieur
Marie Thérèse de la Sablière,
Hersart du Buron, Messieur
Driennays, le Comte et la Com
Comtesse de Kerret et leurs fill
et leurs enfants, le Comte et la Com
Général et Madame de Biré et
de Kérouallan, le Comte de B
ses enfants, la Comtesse Alfred de
de Beaumont, la Marquise de
Blois et ses enfants, le Marquis
Ont l'honneur de vous faire
viennent de faire en la personne

Marie Marguerite Félicité

Vicomtesse de Kerret,

leur mère, grand'mère, arrière grand'mère, tante, grand'tante et cousine, décédée à Paris, au Couvent des Sœurs de l'Espérance le 17 Mai 1893, dans sa quatre-vingt-cinquième année, munie des Sacrements de l'Église.

Priez pour Elle!

Monsieur
et Madame Hadley
93 Whitney avenue New Haven
Connecticut
Amérique

An example of Victorian-era mourning stationery. The thickness of the black edge bars on the letter and the envelope denote the death was a very close relative.

THE RETURN OF THE GOTHIC SKULL

Mourning items that incorporated motifs of skulls and skeletons, though less common than the more widely used symbols like weeping willows and urns, brought a stark and haunting beauty to the grief rituals in this era. These macabre symbols, extremely popular due to the Gothic era's fascination with death and the afterlife, on occasion found their way onto decorative objects, imbuing them with a profound and eerie elegance.

Some families were, reportedly, in possession of 'mourning clocks'. These timepieces often featured intricately designed faces with miniature skulls marking the hours. The hands of the clock might be shaped like skeletal fingers, their slow, relentless movement a constant reminder of the passage of time and the inevitability of death. The clock case was often adorned with carvings of skulls and crossbones, sometimes intertwined with more traditional mourning symbols like ivy, representing eternal life. Although there is little proof that these items existed, the sad hour clock is actually a metal plaque/coffin plaque embossed in the shape of a clock face with the clock hands set to the time of death of the deceased. It was thought that if time continued, the deceased would linger.

The mourning brooch and mourning rings were other captivating examples. While many Victorians featured more subdued designs on their jewelry, some daringly incorporated skull and skeleton motifs. Often made of jet or onyx, these pieces might display a small, intricately carved skull at their centre, surrounded by delicate filigree work or framed by black enamel. Skeleton figures, sometimes posed in contemplative stances or holding hourglasses, could be seen etched into the surface or molded in relief. These brooches were worn as bold statements of mourning.

Personal accessories such as handkerchiefs and fans, as discussed, sometimes bore these macabre motifs. Handkerchiefs were used to dab away tears, and might be embroidered with delicate skulls or tiny skeletons dancing along the edges. Mourning fans, typically sombre in their design, occasionally featured painted scenes of skeletons or skulls interwoven with traditional mourning symbols.

Even household items were not immune. Decorative vases, for instance, might feature skeletal hands or skull motifs amid more traditional floral designs. These vases, often placed in parlours or mourning rooms, blended the beauty of nature with the inevitability of death, creating a juxtaposition that was both unsettling and thought-provoking. Similarly, mirror frames adorned with skull and skeleton carvings added a Gothic touch to Victorian interiors, their reflections serving as a daily reminder of the thin veil between life and death.

A multimedia memorial hair art incorporating memorial symbols, an anchor, a palm tree and a cross.

MEMORIAL HAIR ART

A Victorian mourning bracelet with a thick band of woven hair, c.1865. It has a pair of tinted photo miniatures of two young girls under glass.

In the labyrinthine halls of Victorian artistry, one of the most poignant and fascinating forms of craftsmanship emerged from the interplay of grief and creativity: memorial hair art. This intricate tradition, often overshadowed by its macabre associations, is a testament to the era's profound engagement with memory, love and the transient nature of life.

Victorian memorial hair art was an exquisite and highly personal form of commemoration. It involved creating intricate designs from the hair of deceased loved ones, transforming what might seem morbid into something beautiful and deeply sentimental. Artisans meticulously wove, braided and sculpted hair into delicate flowers, leaves and other natural motifs, framed or encased in jewelry and other keepsakes. The hair, preferably blonde or auburn, due to its resilience over time, served as a lasting physical link to the departed.

The framed flower motif is one of the most striking examples of this artistry. In these pieces, hair was fashioned into detailed floral arrangements, often set against a dark background to enhance the contrast. The flowers symbolized various aspects of Victorian sentimentality. Among the most popular, roses represented love and mourning, lilies stood for purity and forget-me-nots conveyed the enduring memory of the deceased. These pieces were typically encased in shadow boxes or under glass, preserving their delicate beauty for generations.

Another compelling form of memorial hair art was the creation of mini cemeteries under a cloche, a bell-shaped glass cover. These three-dimensional scenes often included tiny tombstones, trees and graveyards. The artistry required to produce such detailed and miniature landscapes was immense. Each element was carefully constructed to maintain the integrity of the hair while creating a realistic, poignant yet perhaps macabre tableau.

The creation of memorial hair art was a highly skilled craft, often undertaken by professional artisans who specialized in this delicate work. These artists needed a deep understanding of hair's properties and how to manipulate it without causing damage. The hair was often boiled and treated to ensure longevity and pliability before weaving into intricate patterns.

At its core, memorial hair art expressed the era's preoccupation with death and remembrance. The Victorians also believed that hair, a part of the body that did not decompose, was an ideal medium for memorialization. It represented a permanent link to the person who had passed away, offering a palpable connection that could be cherished and passed down through generations.

The tools of the trade were as specialized as the craft itself. Tiny needles, fine threads, and magnifying glasses were essential for creating the minute details that characterized these pieces. The process was time-consuming and required immense patience and precision, qualities that were greatly admired in Victorian society.

Interestingly, not all hair used in these artworks came from the deceased. Sometimes, hair from living family members was included in a piece, symbolizing the ongoing bond between the living and the dead. This practice highlighted the Victorian belief in the continuity of relationships beyond death.

The prevalence of memento mori keepsakes in the Victorian era can be attributed to a confluence of factors, and served as constant reminders of life's fragility, the inevitability of death and the hope of an afterlife, encapsulating the complex relationship between the Victorians and their mortality. ❀

A memorial picture with an angel and real hair c.1850.

CHAPTER IX

The HOUSE *of* SHADOWS

FROM HOME TO FUNERAL HOME

A HOME DRAPED IN BLACK

A stately residence stands in the heart of London, nestled among the cobblestone streets and gaslit alleys. The architecture is a testament to the wealth and status of its owners. Yet, on a chilly November morning, a sombre transformation begins as news of a family death spreads through the household. The once vibrant home now becomes a place of mourning.

The first and most immediate task is draping black crepe over the mirrors and portraits. This is not merely for the aesthetics; it is a solemn act based on the belief that the soul of the deceased might become trapped within the mirrored surfaces, unable to move on to the afterlife. The portraits of the deceased are cloaked in darkness, another visual reminder of their departure.

The drawing room, often the centre of the family's social life, undergoes a profound transformation into a mourning parlour. Heavy black curtains replace the usual light drapes, blocking out the sunlight. Previously adorned with rich, colourful fabrics, the furniture is shrouded in black coverings. An ebony coffin is placed in the centre of the room, surrounded by an array of melancholy floral arrangements – lilies, chrysanthemums and laurel, all chosen for their association with death and remembrance. The scent of the flowers mixes with the smell of embalming fluid and decay, creating an unsettling atmosphere of reverence, sorrow and the reminder of one's physical mortality.

Every aspect of the house serves as a symbol of mourning. The clocks are stopped at the hour of death, for some, a gesture meant to signify the suspension of everyday life; for others, it is their belief that time stops at the moment of death, and if time continues, the spirit of the deceased will haunt the living. For whichever reason, the clocks are restarted after the funeral. Quietly the family and visitors enter and exit through the back door.

The extremely grand American homes of the nineteenth century had 'death doors' placed off the parlour that led outside, without a set of steps, providing an accessible and appropriate means of getting the deceased out of the home. In nineteenth-century Europe and America, the deceased were always carried out of the house feet first so they wouldn't look back into the house and beckon a living family member to join them into the hereafter.

Superstitions continued to play a significant role, with windows cracked open to allow the soul of the deceased to depart and a wreath of laurel and yew, symbols of immortality and sorrow, hanging on the front door to signal the household's bereavement to the outside world.

In the days following the death, the house is filled with visitors paying their respects. They enter the dimly lit parlour and offer condolences to the family. Guests, dressed in mourning attire, speak in hushed tones, their conversations punctuated by the occasional sob or prayer.

Refreshments are served – simple biscuits and tea, devoid of the usual finery and flair. It is a time for reflection and quiet support, the community coming together to share in the family's grief.

Larger funeral procession including a double horse drawn cortege in a London suburb c.1890.

The household now operates under the solemn rules of mourning. Social engagements are put on hold; the family abstains from public gatherings, theatre and concerts. Even the children, in their mourning attire, replace their usual lively play with quieter, more subdued activities. Meals are taken with a solemn air. Like the rest of the house, the dining room is draped in black, and the usual cheerful banter is replaced by quiet conversations and shared memories of the departed.

As months pass, the strictures of mourning gradually ease. The heavy black drapes are replaced with lighter fabrics, and the family begins to reintroduce colour into their clothing and surroundings. They transition with a wardrobe now including shades of grey and mauve.

Over time, the house, once shrouded in sorrow, begins to regain its former vibrancy. Yet, it retains the quiet dignity of a family that has mourned deeply and loved dearly.

DYING IN THE LIVING ROOM

A casket displayed in a working class home. Oddly the coffin is placed near the coal heater.

In the Victorian era, the parlour was the heart of the home, serving as a multifunctional space for receiving guests, entertaining, and mourning deceased family members. But as the twentieth-century loomed, a wave of societal changes, including the professionalization of funeral services and the increasing prominence of hospitals as the primary place of death, began to reshape cultural attitudes. These shifts significantly contributed to the diminishing role of the home as the central space for mourning.

The advent of funeral parlours and mortuaries presented families with a new option for hosting wakes and viewings. These professional establishments, coupled with the increasing number of deaths occurring outside the home in hospitals, further distanced the domestic space from the rituals of death.

There are countless articles citing explanations for the rather colourful emergence of the 'living room' as a term to replace the word 'parlour' or, more specifically, the dramatic 'death room'. The term 'death room' allegedly comes in response to the Victorians using the parlour as a room to lay out their dead. Many articles credit an early twentieth-century issue of *Ladies Home Journal* declaring that it should no longer be referred to as a parlour or a death room, but rather a 'living room' – the parlour had evolved into a space focused on the living, hence the change in name.

Although this would be another lovely conversation starter, it is a passionately embraced fallacy. However, Edward Bok, the editor of *Ladies Home Journal* (1839–1919) did lobby for redefining domestic spaces, including promoting the term 'living room'. The term existed long before the twentieth-century, with the *Oxford English Dictionary* citing its earliest known use in 1787 from the *World & Fashionable Advertiser*. In addition, although death was an all-too-common occurrence, the use of the parlour as a 'death room' could not have been so frequent within one family that its primary use was that of a make-shift funeral home/parlour.

MES CHAGRINS LES PLUS PROFONDS (MY DEEPEST SORROWS)

French funeral etiquette and mourning in the late 1800s had many similarities with most of the Western world, but there were some unique differences from those of England and the United States. French law played a significant role in someone's death and only permitted a corpse to be displayed by the family for no more than three days after passing on. Their reasoning was 'lack of ice',[22] although it is hard to imagine that they had any less ice than the rest of Europe. Thus, as per an article appearing in the *Dundee Evening Telegraph* of 1877 the people of France were alerted to the mandate with, 'three days [was] consequently the outside limit of time that the law of hygiene and the rules of common sense [could] allow [for] family affection[23].

A studio portrait featuring a well-dressed woman in mourning wear, Paris, c.1908.

Upon the certification of a loved one's passing, the family's first formal step was to notify the mayoralty in the *arrondissement* (a city municipal district) where the deceased person lived. This office, upon receiving the notification, dispatched a government-sanctioned physician to examine the corpse and determine the cause of death. The family then had to have an act of decease drawn up, an official document confirming the person's death. Only after this document was completed and filed, did the mayor assign the day and hour for the funeral, ideally accommodating the wishes of the deceased person's family.

While the body was on display and yet to be interned, no one in the family was to speak above a whisper while at home. The family did not eat together but instead dined alone in their bedrooms or some other private room. On the day of the funeral, 'the *porte-cochère* (entranceway) of the house wherein the apartment of the deceased [was] situated [was] draped with black, and all other persons who [had] apartments in the same building . . . abstain[ed] from receiving visitors.[24]

For a French widow, the mourning period was not just a personal choice but also a legal obligation. It was against the law for a widow to marry less than ten months after her husband's death. If she did remarry, her dress was expected to be simple and not white. Even if the remarriage occurred within a year of her husband's death, she could only lay her widow's weeds aside for the ceremony itself but was expected to immediately resume them afterwards, her new spouse going into mourning with her out of respect. A French widower, however, had no legal obligation to wait to remarry, although he did have an ethical/moral responsibility to wait at least six months.

PRESERVING THE MEMORIES AND THE DEAD

Up until the late 1800s, the duty of preparing the deceased for viewing and burial most often fell upon the shoulders of the family and other community members. This would be the local 'layer out' – usually a woman or group of women who would assist with carrying out the 'last offices' and attend to the grieving family and the deceased's needs. The body would be washed, dressed and laid out in a coffin built by the local cabinet maker and placed in the centre of the parlour, propped up slightly within anticipation of the wake and for mourners' visits. The term 'wake' is believed to be a derivative from the Old English word 'wacan' that means to become awake and the Proto-Germanic word 'wakjaną' which translate to awaken.

The reason for a wake is in dispute. Some researchers state the body needed to be closely observed for three days to make sure the person didn't wake from a deep sleep or illness before the burial; others assert the body needed to be watched over to protect it from resurrectionists, while the accepted modern reason is it is to allow immediate and extended family and friends to pay their last respects.

By the mid-1800s, there was a slight shift of duties, with the cabinet makers/coffin-builders beginning to assist with funeral transportation, assuming the role of 'undertaker' and eventually as a funeral director and assuming the important duty of embalming. Although embalming methods have existed for thousands of years, dating back to the Egyptians, arterial embalming appears to have first appeared in eighteenth-century England. The technique was developed in the early seventeenth-century by the English physiologist William Harvey, who experimented with injecting coloured solutions into the arteries of cadavers. By using these solutions, he aimed to visually trace the flow of blood through the body, providing clearer evidence for his groundbreaking discovery that blood circulates in a closed system, rather than being consumed by tissues as was previously believed. Later, anatomist Frederik Ruysch and scientist Gabriel Clauderus are believed to have used similar arterial injection techniques to prevent cadavers from decomposing.

Ruysch's astonishing anatomical tableaux combined scientific curiosity with artistic expression. His compositions featured fetal skeletons, arteries, veins, capillaries and even gallstones, arranged in intricate, almost whimsical dioramas. The fetal skeletons were posed in human-like scenes – sometimes appearing to mourn, holding flowers or playing musical instruments. He used preserved human tissue, like veins and arteries, as decorative elements, arranging them to resemble weeping willows or other natural forms. One of Ruysch's most unique dioramas includes a fetal skeleton wiping a tear from their eye, using their placenta as a handkerchief. Ruysch's work was a blend of the macabre and the beautiful, offering both a scientific examination of human anatomy and a reflection on life's fleeting essence. His meticulous preservation techniques using secret embalming fluids gave these displays an almost lifelike appearance.

The most practical and modern development of arterial embalming ushered to the masses was from an eighteenth-century Scottish anatomist named William Hunter. He is credited with being the first person to successfully execute a full arterial and cavity embalming as a way to preserve a body for eventual burial. Hunter's accomplishments gained nationwide attention in 1775 via Martin Van Butchell, an eccentric dentist. Butchell reached out to Hunter's brother, John, requesting he embalm his dead wife. In addition to the conventional embalming, John was asked to add colour additives to create a glow on the corpse's cheeks, dress her in her wedding gown, implant a set of glass eyes, embed her in a layer of plaster of Paris and display her in a glass-topped coffin in the family's living room. Allegedly, this was all done in response to a clause in his marriage

Martin van Butchell, the eccentric dentist, had his wife embalmed and kept in the front room of his home for years.

settlement that allowed him access to her property and wealth only while she remained above ground.

Van Butchell's past antics led many to believe that the embalming was a mere publicity stunt. However, the public's fascination with the unusual request was so intense that Van Butchell was compelled to place a formal ad in the *St James Chronicle*. The ad only added to the controversy. It read: 'Van Butchell (not willing to be unpleasantly circumstanced and wishing to convince some good minds that they have been misinformed) acquaints the Curious, no stranger can see his embalmed wife, unless (by a Friend personally) introduced to himself, any day between Nine and One, Sundays excepted.'

THE PROCESS

Although the reasoning behind Hunter performing the Van Butchell embalming was peculiar, his procedure was standard for the period. The process of arterial embalming begins with draining the blood from the circulatory system to ensure the effective distribution of the embalming fluid and reduce the skin from discolouration. This typically started with the carotid artery, although other arteries could also be used. A small incision was made to expose the artery, and a cannula or tube was inserted. Embalming fluid, which commonly included a mixture of arsenic, zinc chloride or later formaldehyde, was injected using a gravity-fed system or a hand-operated pump. The fluid travelled through the arterial system, displacing blood and diffusing into the tissues, thereby preserving them.

After arterial injection, the body cavities required additional treatment to prevent decomposition. Additional liquids and air needed to be removed, and this involved making a small incision in the abdomen and using a trocar, a sharp-pointed instrument, to puncture the internal organs and specific sections of the bloated body to release 'corpse gas' and fluids. The body was then opened, removing particular organs, and the cavity was filled with a more robust preservative solution, which was then sent through the arteries in an effort to guarantee thorough preservation.

Once the embalming process was complete, the incisions were sutured and the body was rewashed. Embalmers would then apply cosmetics to restore a lifelike appearance, use specialized instruments for 'setting the features', and address any discolouration or swelling that occurred during the process. Some practitioners began the process by securing the mandible (jaw) shut with wire, while others waited till just before the cosmetic stage.

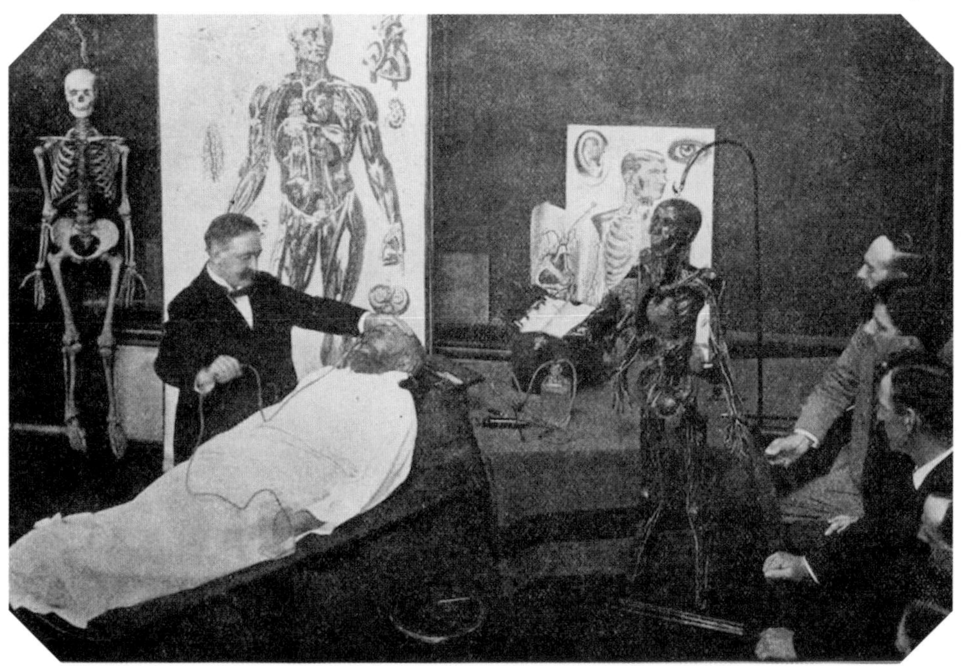

An early embalming class illustrating injecting the embalming fluid through the cadaver's eye.

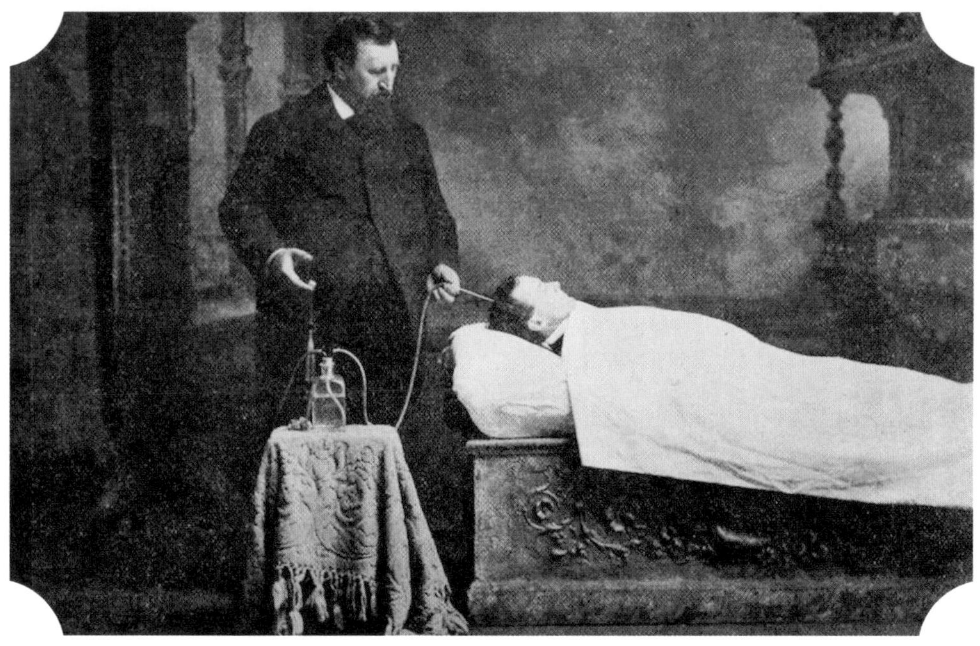

A representative from the Champion Company demonstrates an embalming process using the Champion needle process.

SIX HUNDRED THOUSAND FALLEN SOLDIERS AND THE RISE OF EMBALMING

In the 1850s, the American Civil War was a bitter conflict between the Northern (Union) and the Southern (Confederacy) states primarily over slavery and states' rights. The war ended in a Union victory, leading to the abolition of slavery and the preservation of the United States as a single nation. It was a watershed moment in many aspects of American history, including the development and popularization of embalming.

Before the Civil War, embalming was a relatively obscure practice, with most Americans opting for swift burials due to the rapid onset of decomposition. Preservation methods were rudimentary, often involving ice or simple chemicals temporarily delaying purification. Some caskets had a 'window' where the head would sit, which allowed for viewing the face of the deceased without opening the casket top and releasing any of the precious cold air. These methods were inadequate for the needs of a nation suddenly faced with transporting the bodies of 600,000 fallen soldiers long distances to their final resting places. This grim reality created an unprecedented demand for effective preservation techniques.

The sheer scale of casualties, combined with the geographical dispersion of battlefields, meant that thousands of families wanted their loved ones returned home for proper burial. Traditional body preservation methods were insufficient for the long journeys from the battlefield to home, often resulting in advanced decomposition that made identification and viewing difficult or impossible. This spurred technological and methodological advancements in embalming, promoting arsenic-based embalming fluids, which effectively preserved bodies for extended periods.

Many factors came into play simultaneously for the concept of embalming to have a significant emotional effect on the era's population. The cultural importance of having a dignified and personal farewell for the deceased became essential to the mourning process. Families wished to honour their loved ones with proper funerals, which often included viewing the body. Embalming made this possible.

The government and military began to recognize its benefits. The body of Colonel Elmer Ellsworth, a friend of President Abraham Lincoln and the first Union officer killed in the war, was embalmed and viewed by thousands. But the man who put embalming on the map was Lincoln, who, while alive, was a staunch advocate: his death did the most for the cause. After being assassinated on 14 April 1865, by John Wilkes Booth, his body was embalmed by Charles Brown, the same man who had embalmed Lincoln's son, Willie. Lincoln's remains were then put on a funeral train that transported them 1,654 miles, travelling through seven states with stops in

A gruesome sight of an American Civil War burial party on a Virginia battlefield, c.1865.

principal cities and state capitals for processions, orations and additional lying in state, before burial in Springfield, Illinois.

By the time Lincoln arrived in New York, rumours began to swirl that the president was looking a bit worse for wear. However, it was still touted as an impressive feat of embalming, and the effort did not go unnoticed by the public, who began to embrace the concept of embalming.

Union dead remain on the battlefield at Gettysburg, 1–3 July 1863. Photographed by Timothy O'Sullivan.

Funeral bearers, or 'mutes,' customarily preceded funeral processions and were a common sight in 19th-century London.

THE BIRTH OF A DYING BUSINESS

Embalming parlours existed in the mid-nineteenth century. However, the majority of postmortem work still took place at the deceased's home. The house-calling embalmer came with an array of portable tools and equipment. This included everything from surgical tools and trocars to a folding cooling table where the embalmer could prepare a corpse. The table could be cleaned and transformed into an elegant viewing table when completed.

In the late 1800s, the United States and Europe saw the establishment of organized cemeteries, which led to a funeral 'industry'. By the end of the century, the cabinet maker, the primary source for coffins, officially began taking on more undertaking roles. This was a direct result of the mass production of coffins, which put a significant dent in the cabinet maker's revenue stream, and it was common for his sideline to include renting horses, buggies and carriages to transport the deceased from the home to the cemetery or from the hospital to the house.

Eventually, the embalming process moved out of the home and into a formal funeral 'home' with a funeral 'parlour', where the embalming was performed in a separate space, usually in the basement. This increased the need for postmortem transportation, a service already being provided by the undertaker, and became an essential service. There now was a need for transportation from homes or hospitals with hearses and ambulances.

Early in the 1900s, undertakers became known as morticians and funeral directors, and the new National Funeral Directors Association encouraged them to become a profession rather than just a trade.

The terms 'embalmer', 'mortician', 'undertaker' and 'funeral director' are often mistakenly interchanged. An embalmer or mortician preserves and prepares the corpse and may perform the work of an undertaker. An undertaker originally referred to coffin-builders who sometimes assisted with funeral transportation – but who may or may not have embalmed bodies or assisted with funeral preparations. The title 'funeral director' describes someone who organizes and manages funerals and who may perform any of the work described above.

Out of greed and necessity, resourceful individuals developed the business of dying into a lucrative profession. The climate was perfect for an industry reliant on death, tradition, vanity and emotion. For the affluent, it relieved them of the 'burden' of all the nasty details one needs to deal with when a loved one dies – notably the corpse. However, it also let them flex their monetary muscle and have a public show of emotion by securing the most extravagant services offered by the funeral home. Lavish flower arrangements, ornate horse-drawn carriages, coffins made from rare wood, and even a pair of 'mutes'.

Mutes were professional mourners hired to stand in solemn silence during funeral processions and ceremonies. They symbolized the depth of the family's grief and added gravitas to the event. Dressed in dark attire with long cloaks, black

Dr. Bunnell's embalming establishment on the edge of the battlefield.

gloves and top hats adorned with crepe, mutes embodied the era's fascination with mourning.

The primary duty of a mute was to maintain a sombre demeanour, serving as a silent reminder of mortality. They typically led the funeral procession, walking slowly and deliberately, sometimes carrying staffs or other symbols of mourning. Their presence was meant to evoke respect and reflection among the attendees and passersby. The use of mutes highlighted the Victorian appreciation for the theatrics of passing on, where appearances and adherence to social etiquette were paramount. However, the reputation of mutes was often less dignified than their role suggested. Many were known for heavy drinking, partly due to the nature of their job, which required them to spend long periods in silence and stillness, often outdoors in inclement weather. Alcohol became a way to cope with the monotony and physical discomfort. This led to a common stereotype of the drunken mute, a figure who, despite his outward appearance of solemnity, was frequently intoxicated.

The dichotomy between their public role and private behavior underscores the complex social dynamics of Victorian funerary practices. While mutes were essential to the pomp and circumstance of nineteenth-century funerals, their personal struggles and vices reveal the human side of these otherwise austere figures. ✤

A group of East Enders gather in front of F. Steward Undertaker to have their photo taken. Apparently Steward's specialty was cheap funerals.

CHAPTER X

SHOOTING *the* DEAD

A FINAL FOCUS

A GRAVE SUBJECT

How the relatives can bear to look upon these photographs I cannot understand, unless they have a peculiar love of the horrible. For my part, I cannot see the necessity of photographing the dead at all. If the departed were truly beloved, nothing that may happen in this world can ever efface the dear features from the mind's eye: it needs not a cold, crude photograph representing the last dreary stage of humanity to recall those lineaments.[25.]
– George Bradford(e).

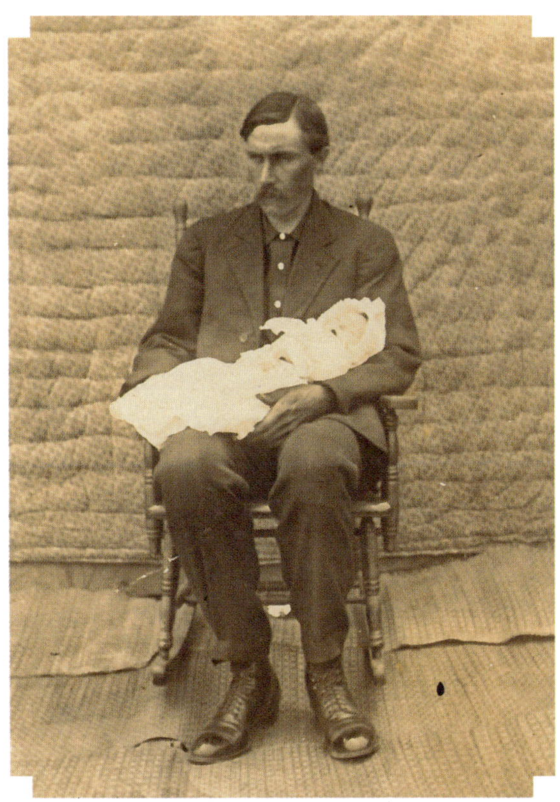

A heart-wrenching cabinet card of a destitute father posing in a makeshift photo studio holding his dead baby.

The excerpt above is from an 1882 article referred to as 'A Grave Subject' [26], written by photographer, cartographer and publisher George Bradford(e), voicing his incomprehension and virtual disgust of Victorians embracing post-mortem photography of their deceased loved ones.

Bradford(e)'s thoughts were those of a minority, since postmortem photography was a phenomenon passionately adopted by his contemporaries. Westerners of this era had a very volatile relationship with death, asking all kinds of questions. Was it beautiful? Was it a painful part of life? Was it just the passing on to a much better place? Was it God's will or the work of an evil entity? One way to try and make sense of it all was to capture it forever, via a two-dimensional photograph mounted to a pocket-sized piece of sturdy cardboard or tin that you could carry next to your heart until you, too, passed.

When the decision was made to employ the services of a photographer to capture images of a deceased loved one, it did not matter that the loved one had already crossed over. Their body was still here, you could see it and touch it, and through the magic of modern technology, the deceased could live forever via a highly polished, silver-plated sheet of copper sensitized with iodine vapours – an 1800s daguerreotype.

THE 'LAST SLEEP'

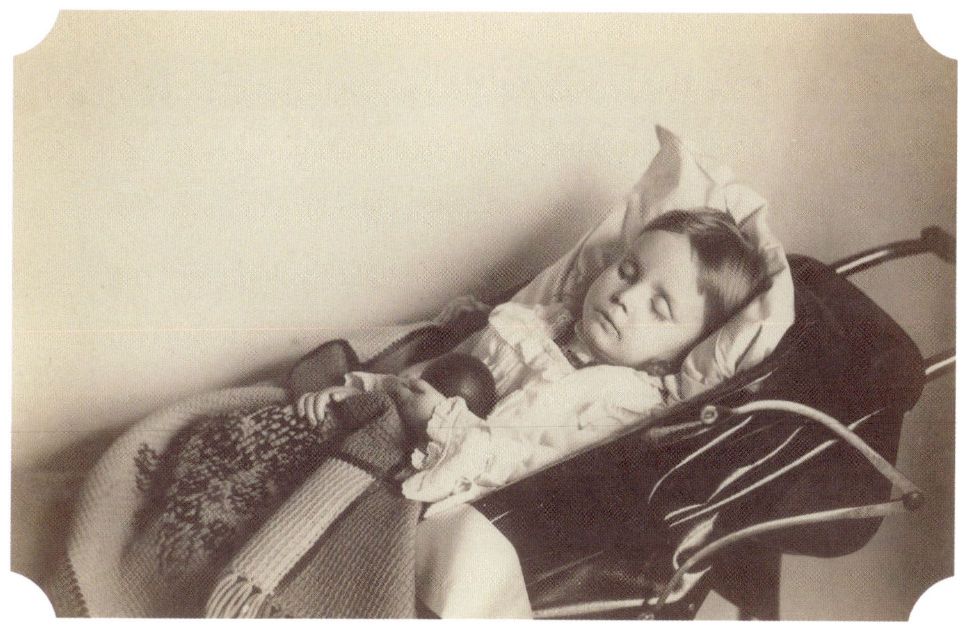

An unique style of post-mortem photography involved deceased children being posed with items they had once enjoyed.

The 'Last Sleep' pose typically presents the deceased lying on a bed or couch, arranged in such a manner that they appear to be merely resting. The eyes are closed, often naturally or with subtle manipulation, to avoid the stark and unsettling gaze that the open eyes of the deceased can present in a photograph or in life. Hands are usually folded, sometimes holding a small memento like a flower or a cherished object, enhancing the illusion of serenity from a painful death. This positioning of the hands also avoids the limpness of the hands after the claw-like effects of rigor mortis have subsided.

Central to the 'Last Sleep' pose is the quest to capture a sense of lifelike tranquility. Photographers of the era took great care in ensuring that the deceased's expression conveyed peacefulness. The mouth might be slightly upturned to suggest a faint smile, and care was taken to smooth out any signs of suffering or

A young girl is casually posed upright in her favourite chair clutching her dolls.

> The overall composition was designed to evoke a sense of calm and repose, with every element carefully chosen to enhance the lifelike quality of the image.

distress that might have been present at the time of death. This meticulous attention to detail was not merely an artistic choice but a deeply empathetic gesture meant to comfort grieving families.

The settings for these photographs were often domestic, reflecting the intimate and personal nature of the practice. The deceased would be arranged in familiar surroundings, in the family home. The use of beds and couches reinforced the notion of tranquil rest and helped integrate the final image into the daily lives of the survivors, providing a comforting sense of continuity. The background might include personal items, family heirlooms or religious artifacts, further placing the deceased within the context of their life and faith.

Lighting played a crucial role in these photographs. Soft, natural light was preferred, casting gentle shadows and highlighting the serene expression of the subject. Photographers employed techniques to ensure the light fell gently on the face, avoiding harsh contrasts of light and shadow. The overall composition was designed ironically to evoke a sense of calm and repose, with every element carefully chosen to enhance the lifelike quality of the image.

Historians categorize many postmortem photos as 'close-ups', when in conventional photographic terms, they would be considered medium shots. These shots are quite haunting, most notably when featuring a young child. The camera is positioned in front of the deceased, over the body and pointed down at a 45-degree angle, creating an image that forces the viewer to stare into the deceased's eyes. Sometimes, they are open, which makes the experience all the more intense.

Although these photos were referred to as "The Last Sleep," they were only some of the first steps taken by a grieving family as they sought comfort from the pain of losing a loved one.

FAMILY PORTRAITS

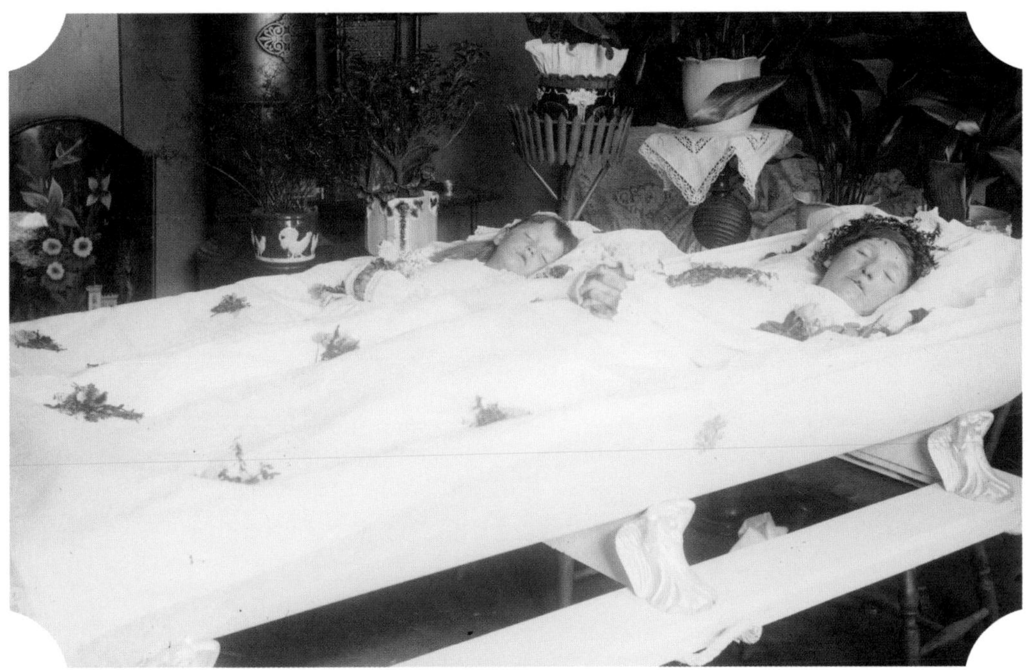

A Danish mother and her daughter are laid out side by side.
We have no information on their case of death.

Contrary to popular belief, the tradition of being photographed in a 'postmortem family portrait' is relatively rare. While there are surviving examples that reflect the desire to preserve the memory of a deceased loved one within what would appear to be a typical family portrait, they are not as common as often suggested. These images are distinctive for their attempt to integrate the departed into a setting that emphasizes continuity with familial bonds despite the finality of death. This style of portraiture captures a moment frozen in time, where the living and the deceased are brought together, creating a lasting memento of connection and unity.

In these family portraits, the deceased might be seated alongside their living relatives, often in a somewhat lifelike pose. If possible, the photographers would frequently place the deceased in the group's centre, which some believe signifies a position of prominence, symbolizing their continued importance and presence within the family, even in death.

Respect and dignity were meticulously woven into the preparation of these portraits. The deceased, adorned in their finest attire, often the same as they wore in life, or a special garment chosen for the occasion, were treated with utmost care. Makeup was delicately applied to restore a lifelike appearance, smoothing away the pallor of death and restoring a natural complexion. Hair was carefully arranged, sometimes adorned with flowers or other meaningful accessories, adding to the sense of dignity and respect.

Overall, the lighting in these photographs was similar to all other postmortem photography: soft and diffused, creating gentle shadows and a harmonious balance between light and dark, helping to gentle the features of the deceased. However, extra careful control of lighting was needed to ensure that the image of the deceased blended seamlessly with the living family members.

The expressions of the living family members were not just a part of the portrait but a significant element that conveyed the enduring strength of family ties. Rather than overt displays of grief, the focus was on composed, solemn expressions that conveyed a sense of reverence and contemplation. This restraint in emotion was intended to highlight the occasion's solemnity and the enduring strength of family ties. The overall atmosphere of the photograph was one of serene remembrance, a quiet acknowledgment of loss tempered by the enduring presence of the deceased.

Like the 'Final Sleep', the settings for these portraits were often carefully chosen to enhance the sense of intimacy and continuity. Family homes, with their familiar furnishings, personal artifacts and religious symbols, provided a backdrop that emphasized the normalcy and warmth of daily life.

The deceased often would have the aid of hidden supports or props to maintain a lifelike pose. The use of such devices was a delicate art, requiring skill and subtlety to ensure the deceased appears natural and at peace. A standard method involved using special stands or braces concealed behind furniture or drapery, which held the body upright and in a pose that conveyed a sense of normalcy. Not true, the previous scenarios are inaccurate. This is another of those well-circulated morbid myths that, although they make for interesting 'facts' to drop at a cocktail party, are entirely false. In the 1830s, the early days of the daguerreotype, exposure times could be up to 90 seconds. That meant a person sitting for a portrait would need to sit or stand motionless for the entire exposure time. To relieve some of the stress of striking a pose for such an extended time, photographers developed props and devices that helped subjects stay stock-still while the long exposure time elapsed. It's these behind-the-scenes photographs of photographers of the time utilizing these posing stands that began the legend of photographers' postmortem tools of the trade. For years, buyers and sellers of antique photography have made false claims that photos of people who were very much alive at the time the photos were taken are, in fact, dead but held up by the "postmortem stand."

These family portraits with the deceased are profoundly evocative, offering a glimpse into how families sought to cope with and memorialize their loss. They provide a powerful testament to the enduring bonds of love and the desire to keep the memory of the departed alive within the family circle. By including the deceased in family portraits, these images transcend the mere documentation of death, becoming a poignant celebration of life, connection, and the resilience of the human spirit. They are profoundly moving and speak volumes about the emotional strength of such families.

FROM THE CRIB TO THE COFFIN

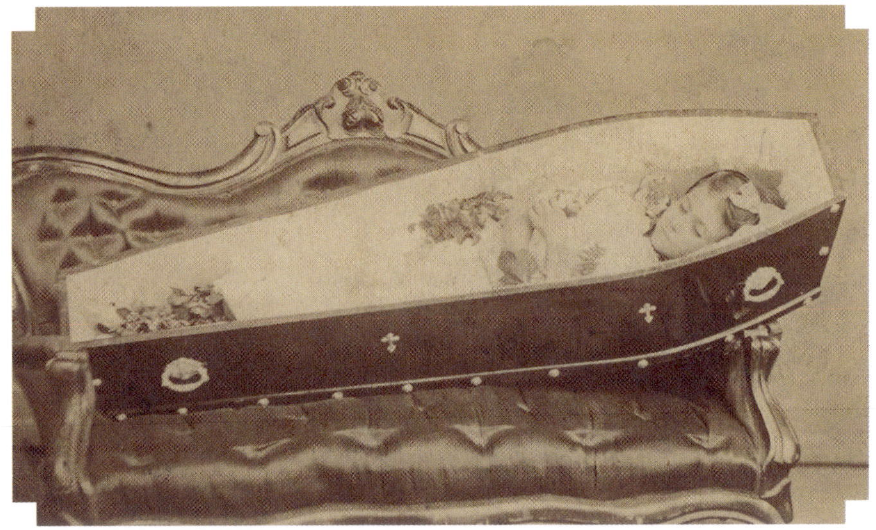

An unique posing of a child in her casket, which is propped up on formal love seat. Perhaps this was her favourite chair.

Unfortunately for many, life's journey from the crib to the coffin was a very short trip. The most tragic and, regrettably, some of the most common examples of postmortem photography from the Victorian era feature infants and children. The reasons so many children died at such an early age were all too numerous. Overcrowded living conditions became highly effective breeding grounds for communicable diseases like measles, rubella, scarlet fever, smallpox and tuberculosis. Epidemics, as we have discussed, periodically ripped through England and the United States, and their favourite victims were infants and young children whose underdeveloped and compromised immune systems were especially vulnerable to infection. During this era, children also faced numerous dangers in the workplace, stemming from hazardous environments, long hours and inadequate protection. Industrialization led to the widespread use of child labour in factories, mines and other dangerous sectors of industry.

The postmortem portraits of children typically depicted the deceased child in an angelic pose, sometimes surrounded by toys, flowers or other sentimental objects; the aesthetic choices in these postmortem photographs were carefully considered to present the child in the Victorian idealization of death as a peaceful sleep. Children were often dressed in their finest clothes, and their bodies were posed to suggest a natural, restful slumber. Flowers symbolized innocence, commonly used as a prop. These flowers were often arranged around the child's body or placed in their hands, enhancing the visual narrative of purity.

Some postmortem photographs went in a peculiar direction, attempting to create the illusion that the child was still alive. In these images, the child might be posed, sometimes appearing to interact with toys or other objects. Photographers used various techniques to achieve this effect, such as propping the child up in a sitting position or arranging their limbs to mimic play. The child's eyes were sometimes artificially opened or, in some cases, painted onto the photograph afterward to enhance the appearance of vitality.

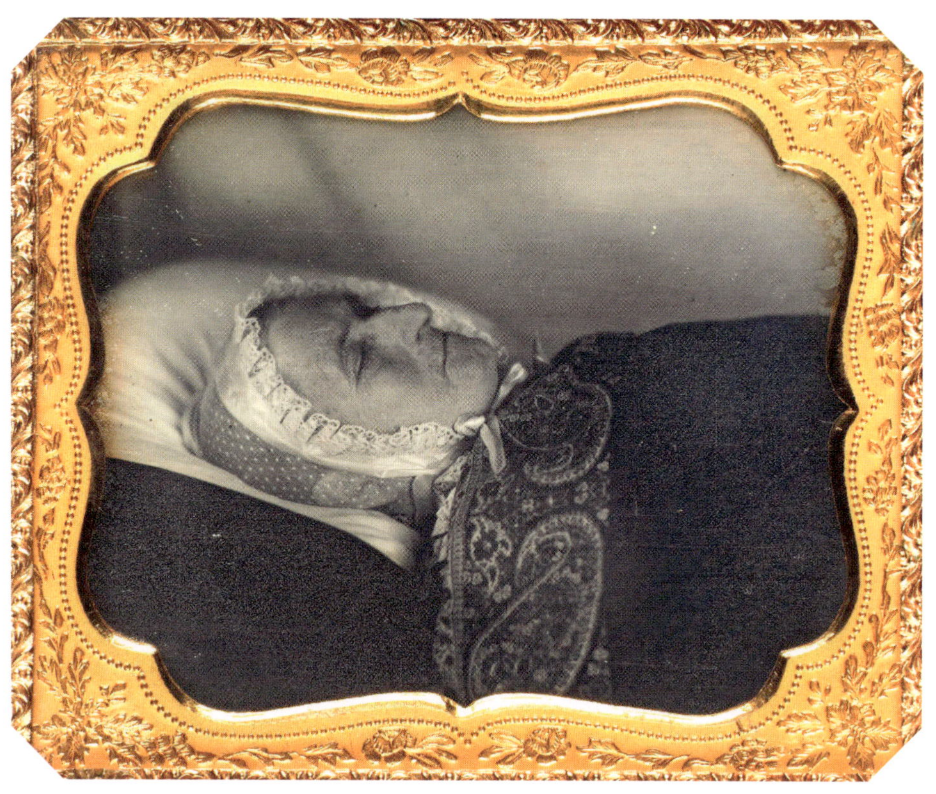

'A long needed rest.' The long exposure time needed with the daguerreotype-process was no issue when photographing the deceased.

A POPULAR PRACTICE

Other than the obvious emotionally charged reasons for having postmortem photographs be part of the mourning process, practical reasons also came into play. The development of the daguerreotype and, later, the *carte de visite* (visiting card) allowed for relatively inexpensive and quick production of photographs. This accessibility helped to popularize the practice across different social classes, making it a widespread phenomenon. However, despite photography coming a long way in the 1800s, it was still a technical operation that needed to be done by a professional, taking home photos was decades away. That meant very few people had pictures of their children opening gifts on holidays or a baby taking their first steps. So, odds were high that if you did not have a portrait of your child taken days before they were to be interred, you would have no physical record of them existing. Thus, the postmortem photograph became a cherished keepsake and a means of coping with grief, providing a way for families to remember and honour their lost children.

During this era, postmortem photography emerged as an intersection of burgeoning photographic art and the deeply ingrained cultural practices surrounding death and mourning. The importance of such images of children can be analyzed from several perspectives, particularly the psychological comfort they provided to grieving families, the role of physical photographs in the mourning process and the broader Victorian attitudes toward death and remembrance.

For parents whose children had died, the sudden absence of a physical presence created a profound emotional void. Postmortem photography addressed this by capturing the image of the deceased child, often depicted as if asleep rather than dead, which provided a visual representation of the child that parents could return to. Psychologically, these photographs served as a concrete connection to the child, mitigating a little of the pain of their physical absence.

The tangibility of these photographs was crucial. Holding a picture allowed parents to engage physically with the memory of their child and played a critical role in the grieving process. Touching the photograph could evoke a sensory memory of the child, making the intangible loss slightly more bearable. Psychological theories suggest that touch is integral to human connection and love: for grieving parents, touching a photograph of their deceased child could serve as a proxy for physical affection, providing solace and a temporary escape from the harsh reality of their loss.

The desire to maintain a bond with the deceased is a powerful aspect of parental love. Victorian postmortem photographs provided a means to sanctify the child's life and affirm their place within the family history. The pictures represented a refusal to let go, a rebellion against the finality of death. By preserving the child's likeness, parents could maintain an relationship with the deceased, incorporating them into the living world through visual representation.

A sister awkwardly holds her deceased sister on her lap for a portrait of the living and the dead.

SURVIVING SIBLINGS IN POSTMORTEM PHOTOGRAPHY

Including surviving siblings in postmortem photographs was a practice that added layers of meaning and emotion to the images. The death of a child was a profound loss. However, the presence of surviving siblings in postmortem photographs provided a way to visually express the family's grief and their continuing bonds with the deceased. Still, it also acknowledged the shared sorrow helped the surviving children understand and process the concept of death.

The photograph became a portrait that celebrated the life of the deceased while highlighting the continuity of the family unit. It conveyed the idea that the deceased child remained an integral part of the family. These images were often staged to reflect a sense of normalcy and peace, with the siblings sometimes holding the deceased child or standing beside them, reinforcing the bond of affection and the permanence of familial ties.

These postmortem images were not just private mementos but also served a social function. They were often displayed prominently in the home, sent to relatives or included in family albums. They created a historical record that future generations could look back on, providing a visual genealogy that preserved the memory of all family members, living and deceased. It allowed descendants to witness the family's history and the impact of loss on the family structure.

The decline of postmortem photography in the late Victorian era can be attributed to several factors. Advances in medicine led to a decline in the overall mortality rate and in 1900, the infant mortality rate had dropped significantly from the 1850s, with estimates suggesting a decline of almost 50%; however, the exact percentage varies depending on the specific region, but the overall trend shows a substantial decrease in infant deaths per 1,000 live births. There was also an altered public perceptions of death, making it less a daily reality and more a medicalized, often sanitized event. Additionally, as photography became more commonplace and less expensive, living portraits became more popular, reducing the necessity for postmortem depictions of loved ones. Instead, funeral photography became more popular, images of the ceremony at which loved ones said goodbye to a body in a coffin. ❀

The shared sorrow helped the surviving children understand and process the concept of death.

CHAPTER XI

TOIL *and* TRAGEDY

WORKING YOURSELF TO DEATH

'AIN'T NO REST FOR THE WEARY' (SWEAT, SOOT, AND SORROW)

A Lewis Hine photograph of a thirteen year-old child labourer in a North Carolina cotton mill.

The Victorian workforce, similar to today's, was basically broken up into four categories: professionals, landowners, wealthy industrialists and labourers, with most of the population falling under the labourer category. As with so many facets of life in the Victorian era, earning a living within a newly created industrialized economy, one that had very little regard for human life, especially if you were poor, could prove hazardous. Ending your 14-hour workday (6 to 7 days a week) with all your limbs intact, or even making it out alive was never guaranteed.

However, when comparing the work environment of today's labourer to one in the late 1800s, the category breakdown is where the similarities end. The Industrial Revolution has been blamed for the introduction of child labour, but unfortunately, that is not accurate. As early as the late 1700s, textile mills in rural England and America commonly had a staff comprising 70 per cent of children. The English historian

E.P. Thompson described these textile factories as 'places of sexual license, foul language, cruelty, violent accidents, and alien manners' [27] and novelist Charlotte Brontë referred to them as the 'soot-vomiting mills' in her 1849 novel *Shirley*. Similarly, chimney sweeps were often boys as young as four years old, used in a filthy and dangerous practice.

However, the industrialization of the West did add some additional unpleasant elements to the child labour situation. The most egregious was the 'hiring' of paupers from the streets and orphanages, where they would be housed, clothed and fed but would receive no wages for their long days at the mill. This virtually stripped them of any identity other than being a 'slave to the mill'.

Of course, children weren't the only victims of the cruelty in the industrialized workplace, and when adults found themselves choosing a career outside the factories, the opportunities available were slim and, many times, even more disgusting and demoralizing.

BLOODSUCKERS

With the period ushering in the birth of 'modern medicine', physicians of the period were obsessed with 'leech therapy'. They prescribed their usage to treat a wide range of maladies, including headaches, bronchitis, reducing fevers and mental health. This led to an ever-increasing need for the nasty little blood suckers and a burgeoning cottage industry.

The harvesting of these disgusting little creatures was primarily done by poor country women who would use their bodies, most notably their legs, as human traps while wading into dirty ponds, hoping to attract a clew (group) of leeches. Once the bloodsuckers attached themselves to the collector's legs, they would be pried off and dropped in a box or pot. Leeches could survive up to 12 months without food and were found in large glass jars on the counters of pharmacies throughout the cities.

Such leech collecting came with danger, however, with the victims suffering excess blood loss, infectious diseases and infections at the blood-sucking sites, which sometimes might have led to a limb being amputated. In rare cases, the infections also led to death.

George Walker, *The Costume of Yorkshire, Leech Finders*, paper and aquatint, 1814.

ONE MAN'S TRASH . . .

Desperate times call for desperate measures, and countless men, women and children were forced to partake in actions that were without question dangerous and demeaning in the effort to make a living. The advent of automation had made its way into specific facets of the economic machine, but there were some unpleasant tasks still requiring a human being to literally dive into the excrement to make a few coins. The segment of society to fill these positions were the poorest, the most uneducated, the booze hounds, the hopheads – and, of course, children.

Mudlarks would scavenge through the low tide waste, which included human excrement, and would be lucky if they made a penny a day selling what they had found. .

THE PURE FINDER: POOP FOR PROFIT

If only the posh women and men of the day knew that the tack for their Arabian horses, the straps on their elegant shoes, the suppleness of their boots, the shine of their handbags and the textured book bindings of their ancient classics were all made with leather that had previously been treated with globs of dog excrement.

The job title 'Pure Finder' has a pleasant ring to it; however, in reality it translated into accumulating dog excrement from the streets of London to sell to tanners. Dog faeces was known as 'pure' since it was utilized in a process by tanners to purify the leather and make it supple.

Pure collectors roamed the streets at night where stray dogs gathered, scooping up faeces and delivering it in the morning to the local tanners. Some collectors wore a glove, usually black, on their scooping hand, but others believed it more challenging to keep a glove clean than a hand and would forgo such protection.

This persistent exposure to dog faeces led to bacterial infections, including campylobacteriosis, salmonella and E. coli. Parasites like Giardia, roundworm, hookworm and tapeworm are present in dog faeces and would find their way into the bodies of the Pure Finders.[29]

Londoners have had a longstanding love–hate relationship with their sewer system, which peaked during the Great Stink and the ensuing cholera epidemic of 1853. Victorian London had a vast network of overworked sewers beneath the city, carrying the effluence of the crowded metropolis down into the Thames.

The Sewer Hunter eked out a living by hunting in the sewers for anything he could sell, Henry Mayhew, 1861.

An unfortunate group of Londoners, known as Toshers, made their living by sifting through raw sewage to find valuables that might have fallen down drains. It was hazardous and disgusting work. The tunnels filled with noxious fumes, forming invisible pockets of deadly gas. Swarms of rats ran through the system and, without warning, the sluices would open, sending torrents of excrement-laden water rushing through the tunnels, washing the Toshers away into the Thames.

The Toshers were easily recognizable. They wore canvas trousers, filthy aprons with multiple large pockets to hold their findings and lanterns strapped to their heads or chests. Some carried long hoes to plow through large piles of excrement in search of something valuable. Eventually, a law was passed in 1841 that prohibited anyone from entering the sewer system without government permission. Surprisingly, toshing was a relatively lucrative endeavour and instead of abandoning their pursuits, the Toshers applied their trade late at night or in the wee hours of the morning.

An offshoot of the Toshers were the mudlarks, often children earning meagre amounts from dredging through the 'gloop' (which included untreated raw sewage and the corpses of humans and animals) lining the shores of the polluted Thames, looking for items of value to sell. Seen as a step down from being a Tosher, they collected anything that could be sold, including rags (for paper making), driftwood (for firewood) and any coins or valuables that might find their way into the river. In addition to being a filthy job exposing the mudlark to countless bacterial infections and viruses, it had the added danger of unpredictable tidal swells of the Thames, resulting in many children being drowned.

A MATCH MADE IN HELL

Who would have thought that the simple matchstick would make certain families of the 1800s millionaires? That it would be the subject of scandal and cover-ups? That it would be the catalyst for the Salvation Army to begin a crusade against the established matchmakers and leave hundreds of men and women with their faces horribly disfigured and others dead?

An English chemist of the 1820s is credited with creating the friction/strike anywhere match. However, it wasn't very reliable until about ten years later, when white phosphorus was added to the tip, which guaranteed a quick strike and a flame-on. There was one small problem: white phosphorus is highly toxic, though it was not known at the time. Years later, when it was determined to be lethal and responsible for killing and disfiguring some of the employees, company

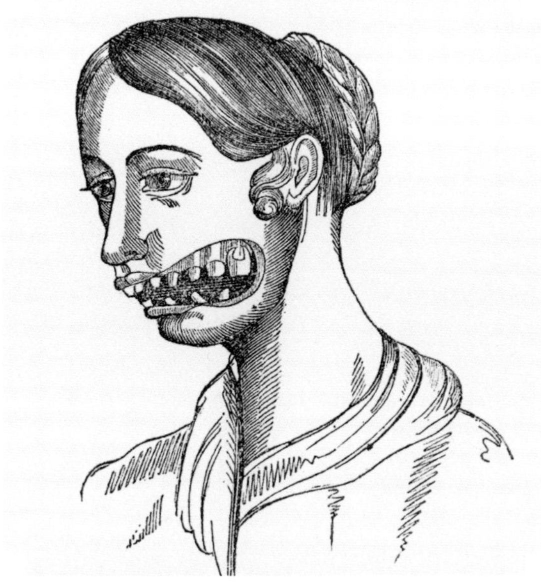

Phossy jaw illustration from a chapter on ulcers of the cheek, *Lectures on the Operations of Surgery*, Liston and Mutter, 1846.

owners ignored the reports. Capitalism was now in full swing.

Thousands of women and hundreds of men worked 12 to 16 hours a day, sitting at long tables and dipping the two ends of finely cut sticks of wood into white phosphorus and then splitting the wood strips into single matches. This work was performed in terrible conditions, with few breaks and the workers were often forced to eat at their workstations. As a result, the toxic phosphorus contaminated their food. If that did not ultimately kill them, it usually led to the development of a dreadful condition known as 'phossy jaw' – phosphorus necrosis of the jaw where the jawbone becomes infected and severely disfigured.

The symptoms, or the horrors, of phossy jaw started with swollen gums and toothaches. Next, an abscess would form, releasing an odorous discharge of pus. The disease would then spread to the surrounding tissue. Tooth loss began as the jawbone started to die, which inevitably led to the removal of the jawbone (in some cases, both the upper and lower jaws). Some dentists even claimed the gums of these patients would glow green in the dark.

Although the condition is known as phossy jaw, the disease is not limited to that area. Other body parts, including the lungs, were also affected, resulting in blood-riddled spittle. It could also cause seizures and meningitis and had a 20 per cent mortality rate.

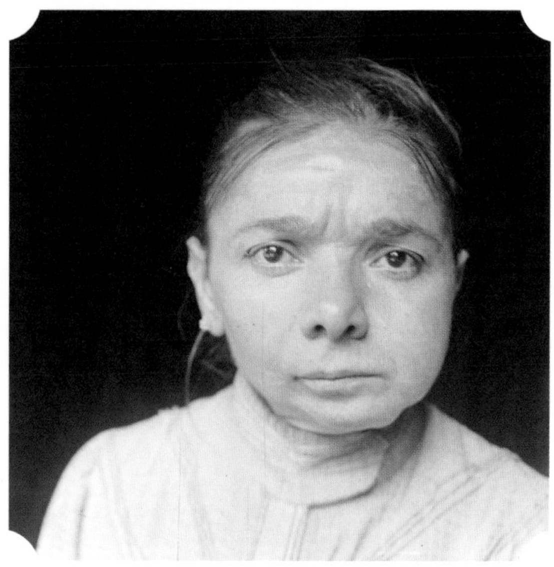

A match factory worker afflicted with 'phossy jaw'.

IT WAS NO MARY POPPINS!

The grimness of William Blake's 'The Chimney Sweep', the tale of a boy sold off into horrible child labour by his father following the death of his mother, is not what we expect when presented with creative works on a chimney sweep. Images of happy, mischievous little boys with dirty faces running through the streets of London, stealing bread from a food cart, or Dick Van Dyke as Bert in the film *Mary Poppins* gleefully singing '*Chim chiminey, chim chiminey, chim chim cher-ee*,'[28] perhaps. A sweep is as lucky as lucky can be is what Hollywood has led us to

Two stereoscopes with true images of the young Victorian-era chimney sweep. A far cry from the character in *Mary Poppins*.

believe was the life of a sweep. However, nothing could be further from the truth.

Tiny children, some as young as four, were seen as the perfect candidates to shimmy down the narrow brick chimneys due to their small stature, and it doesn't take much to imagine how dangerous and dirty such a job was. Their arms and legs were a map of scrapes, cuts and callouses from navigating the tight, claustrophobic spaces. The air was filled with dust and smoke, leading to severe and irreversible lung damage over time.

The smallest and most agile children were in high demand, leading to a cruel practice of deliberately underfeeding some to ensure they remained small enough for the job. By age ten, most had outgrown their usefulness as chimney sweeps. Tragically, some children became trapped in the chimneys or were too frightened to climb. The bosses often would light fires beneath, forcing them to climb out through the top or die of smoke inhalation. An 1840 law aimed to end this brutal practice by making it illegal for anyone under 21 to clean chimneys. However, in the shadowy corners of this Dickensian world, some unscrupulous individuals continued to exploit young sweeps, sending countless young children to an early death.

RATS, RATS, RATS

Overcrowding and poor to non-existent waste management led to a vermin issue for many newly industrialized cities in England and the United States, and a mischief (an antiquated term that refers to a 'pack of rats') of rats scurrying down a street or alley was not an uncommon sight in the nineteenth century. However, in addition to the offensiveness of the rodents free rein, they were also perfect hosts for carrying diseases like Leptospirosis, Salmonellosis, Hantavirus, Sylvatic Typhus, and, of course, the plague into the homes of the public.

A portrait of a New York rat-catcher. The text on the photo reads: 'The kill' - rats killed by ferrets.

Apparently, it was easier to send men out into the streets with a trap, a sack and a ferret to round up the millions of rats that infested the city than to institute a civil and sanitary way of disposing of one's rubbish. Hence, the position of rat-catcher was born.

Small dogs or ferrets assisted the rat-catchers as they searched the filthy streets and homes of Victorian Britain and the United States, looking for the nasty vermin. Ideally, the rat-catcher wanted to capture his prey alive to sell them to an unscrupulous group known as 'ratters' who threw the rats into a pit where a dog was set loose upon them. Spectators placed bets on the length of time it would take the canine to kill the entire mischief.

Catching rats was a dangerous business, however – not only did the vermin harbour disease, like the Black Death, but their bites could cause deadly infections. Yet the position was seemingly prestigious. One of the most famous Victorian rat-catchers, Jack Black, worked for Queen Victoria. In an 1851 interview with the *London Labour*, he revealed his use of massive cages that allowed rats to live for days as long as he fed them; otherwise, they would begin eating one another. He went on to say:

'I've been bitten nearly everywhere, even where I can't name to you, sir, and right through my thumb nail too, which, as you see, always has a split in it, though its years since I was wounded. When a rat's bite touches the bone, it makes you faint in a minute, and it bleeds dreadful – ah, most terrible – just as if you had been stuck with a penknife. You couldn't believe the quantity of blood that come away, sir.'[28]

THE HYPOCRISY OF SEX

Attitudes toward sex in the Victorian era were easily summed up as conflicting and hypocritical. Chastity and modesty were paramount for women, especially those of the middle and upper classes. They were expected to embody physical and moral purity, often reduced to symbols of domestic virtue. In contrast, men were not held to the same standards; sexual freedom was tacitly accepted for them, in and outside of marriage. Prostitution flourished, and men's extramarital affairs were often overlooked or excused as natural male behaviour.

Despite these heavy-handed moral mandates, women turned to sex work for the same reasons they do today: financial necessity and a lack of alternative opportunities. Victorian women faced significant barriers, including limited job prospects, misogyny, restricted access to education and the societal expectation that they should be married in order to be considered respectable. Without a husband, many women found themselves marginalized and without a viable means of support.

Faced with the dire choice between starvation and sex work, many opted for the latter to provide for themselves and their children. While some women found employment in upscale brothels, the majority were left to navigate the perilous streets alone. Tragically, rape often pushed women into sex work. In Victorian England, rape was not recognized as a crime but rather as a scandal

A studio glamour portrait of Cora Pearl lying in a hammock, France (c.1862). Pearl hit her height of fame during the Second Empire period and the beginning of the French Third Republic.

that could ruin a woman's reputation. Victims were often ostracized, and with few options, many turned to selling their bodies, particularly if they bore an illegitimate child as a result of the assault.

Men and young boys also engaged in sex work, though brothels catering to gay men were rare. Like their female counterparts, they faced significant risks, including violence and murder, with little to no protection from the authorities. Sexually transmitted infections, such as syphilis, were widespread and typically untreatable, adding to the dangers of the trade. The infamous case of Jack the Ripper underscores the peril sex workers faced. The Ripper's brutal murders highlighted the vulnerability of sex workers and the general indifference of society to their plight. ❀

Sexually transmitted infections, such as syphilis, were widespread and typically untreatable, adding to the dangers of the trade.

A graphic interpretation of what an unknown French photographer believes goes on in a brothel c.1900.

CHAPTER XII

TWIN SHADOWS

THE BUTCHER AND THE BUNCO ARTIST

WELCOME TO WHITECHAPEL

Serial killing has long fascinated and horrified society, particularly when such murders occur in densely populated cities. These settings, bustling with anonymity, provide a unique environment for killers to operate undetected while allowing them to revel in the chaos they create. Psychologists have commented that rapidly developing cities with a population explosion often lead to feelings of alienation and detachment, both for the predator and the prey.

London in the late nineteenth century was a city grappling with rapid industrialization, overcrowding and a socio-economic divide, leaving specific neighbourhoods neglected, teeming with poverty and vice and creating the perfect environment for a murderous scenario to play out. Similarly, cities in the United States such as New York, Chicago and Boston experienced explosive growth during this era. With their waves of immigration, unregulated expansion and rising crime rates, American urban centers mirrored London's dysfunction – offering the same shadowy corners, transient populations and overwhelmed law enforcement that serial offenders could exploit with ease.

Unfortunately, the moon glistened brightest off the cold steel of a killer's blade in Whitechapel of 1888, one of London's poorest and most overcrowded districts. A melting pot of immigrants and working-class citizens already plagued with inadequate housing and rampant poverty, its dark, narrow streets and poorly lit buildings made it a haven for illicit activity. Prostitution was common, especially among the women struggling to survive. It was in this bleak backdrop that the murders took place, and these conditions played a crucial role in the narrative around the killings. The same could be said of America's rising cities, where similar murders would later unfold, rooted in the grim realities of urban life.

Annie Chapman (September 8, 1888). The second victim of the Jack the Ripper.

THE HORROR BEGINS

On the night of 31 August 1888, Mary Ann Nichols, a 43-year-old woman, was last seen alive at around 2.30 a.m. on the corner of London's Whitechapel Road. She had been turned away from a lodging house because she didn't have the money for a bed. A couple of hours later, her body was discovered by a cart driver named Charles Cross on Buck's Row (now Durward Street). Nichols had been brutally attacked: her throat was cut twice, her abdomen slashed open. Detectives at the crime scene noted that despite the savage wounds, there was little blood splatter, suggesting the killing had been swift and precise.

Just eight days later, on 8 September 1888, Annie Chapman, aged 47, was found murdered. Chapman had been staying at a lodging house on Dorset Street and was last seen alive at 5.30 a.m., speaking with a man on Hanbury Street. Her body was discovered shortly afterwards in the backyard of 29 Hanbury Street. Like Nichols, Chapman's throat had been deeply cut. However, the mutilations to her body were even more grotesque: her abdomen had been cut open, her intestines pulled out and placed over her shoulder. Additionally, her uterus had been removed. This curious fact led investigators to believe the killer may have had some anatomical knowledge.

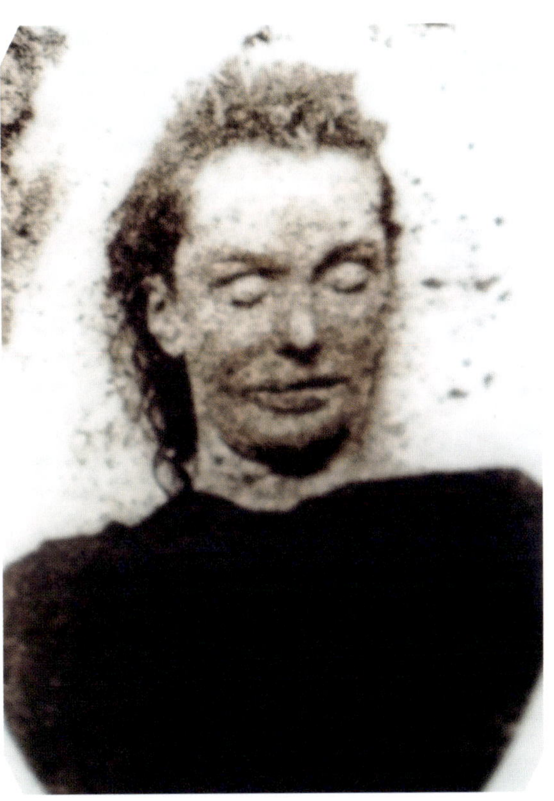

Mortuary photograph of Elizabeth Stride.
A suspected victim of the unidentified Jack the Ripper.

DEAR BOSS

After this second murder, the London police department was flooded with letters, each one claiming to have answers to the grisly murders haunting Whitechapel. Most were dismissed, scrawled by cranks or fearful citizens desperate to name a killer. But one letter, dripping with the stench of arrogance and menace, caught the eye of Detective Abberline. The red ink stood out, a mockery of the blood spilled on the smog-laden streets.

'Dear Boss' it began, the tone disturbingly playful for the horrors it referenced. The author taunted the police, gleeful over their inability to catch him, promising more murders and laughing at their incompetence. It ended with the most chilling signature: 'Jack the Ripper'.

The name itself was a revelation, as sharp as the knife that had taken so many lives. Until now, the killer had been a faceless phantom, but here, in those three words, he had given himself a twisted identity. The letter was handed over to the media, and soon the name spread like wildfire through London's streets. 'Jack the Ripper' became more than just a killer. He was a symbol of terror, a figure lurking in every shadow. The press had its headline, London its monster. The name stuck, seared into the minds of a city already gripped by fear, as Jack continued to haunt the darkness, now a legend in ink and blood.

Dear Boss 25. Sept. 1888.
I keep on hearing the police have caught me but they wont fix me just yet. I have laughed when they look so clever and talk about being on the right track. That joke about Leather Apron gave me real fits. I am down on whores and I shant quit ripping them till I do get buckled. Grand work the last job was. I gave the lady no time to squeal. How can they catch me now. I love my work and want to start again. You will soon hear of me with my funny little games. I saved some of the proper red stuff in a ginger beer bottle over the last job to write with but it went thick like glue and I cant use it. Red ink is fit enough I hope ha. ha. The next job I do I shall clip the ladys ears off and send to the

A photo of the original 'Dear Boss' letter, postmarked 25 September 1888.

The police later determined that the 'Dear Boss' letter was written by a journalist to keep the story alive and increase newspaper sales. Thomas Bulling, a reporter for the Central News Agency, and Fred Best, another journalist, were both considered possible perpetrators. The London police eventually released a statement that they believed the 'Dear Boss' letter a hoax, but the police's suspicions received little publicity, and the public continued to believe the press articles about the true source of the letter.

TWICE THE TERROR

The third murder, that of Elizabeth Stride, occurred on 30 September 1888. Stride, 45, was discovered at around 1 a.m. in Dutfield's Yard, off Berner Street. Her throat had been slashed, but unlike the other victims, she showed no signs of mutilation. This led some to believe the Ripper had been interrupted before he could complete his attack. A witness, Israel Schwartz, had seen Stride with a man shortly before her murder, suggesting that the killer may have fled when he saw Schwartz.

However, the interruption didn't stop him for long. Just 45 minutes after Stride's body was found, the Ripper struck again. Catherine Eddowes, aged 46, was killed in Mitre Square, just a short distance away. Her body was discovered at 1.45 a.m., her throat slashed, and her face severely mutilated. The killer had also disembowelled her, much like Chapman, and had removed her kidney and part of her uterus. Eddowes's murder was notable for the gruesome mutilations and the fact that the killer left behind a piece of her apron, which was later found near a message scrawled in chalk that read: '*The Juwes are the men that will not be blamed for nothing*.' The exact meaning of this phrase remains a subject of debate.

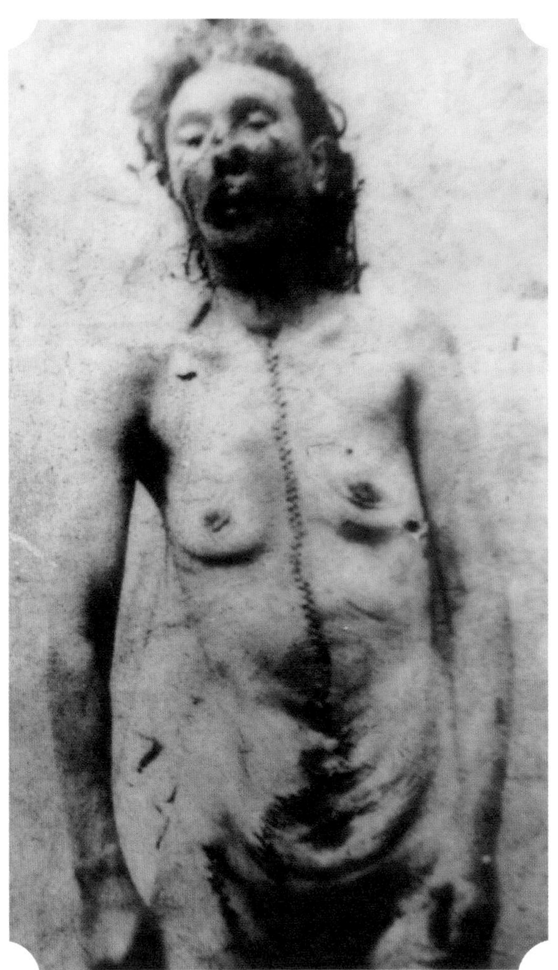

The remains of Catherine 'Kate' Eddowes. She is believed to be the fourth victim of Jack the Ripper.

FROM HELL

The grip of terror escalated as the murders were sensationalized by the press, with newspapers publishing graphic descriptions of the bodies and gory details about the killings. The press coverage made the figure rise to mythic proportions, often stoking fears of a monstrous, inhuman killer. Although the first four victims of Jack the Ripper were confined to prostitutes, their gruesome deaths struck fear in all Londoners, believing that this methodical and sadistic killer might at any moment switch his preferred choice of victims to them.

On 16 October 1888, the Ripper Case took an even more unsettling turn when a letter addressed to George Lusk, head of the Whitechapel Vigilance Committee, arrived at police headquarters. Deemed the 'From Hell' letter because those words were written in the top corner of the note, unlike the numerous hoax letters received by police and press during the Whitechapel murders, it stands out due to its chilling tone and the inclusion of a human kidney fragment. The writer of the letter claimed to have 'fried and ate' half of the kidney of one of his victims.

The Metropolitan Police and City of London Police continued their extensive investigations, but the Ripper's ability to evade capture led to a growing sense of panic and frustration. The use of criminal profiling and forensic investigation techniques was still in its infancy, and despite interviewing hundreds of suspects and offering rewards, the police were at a loss.

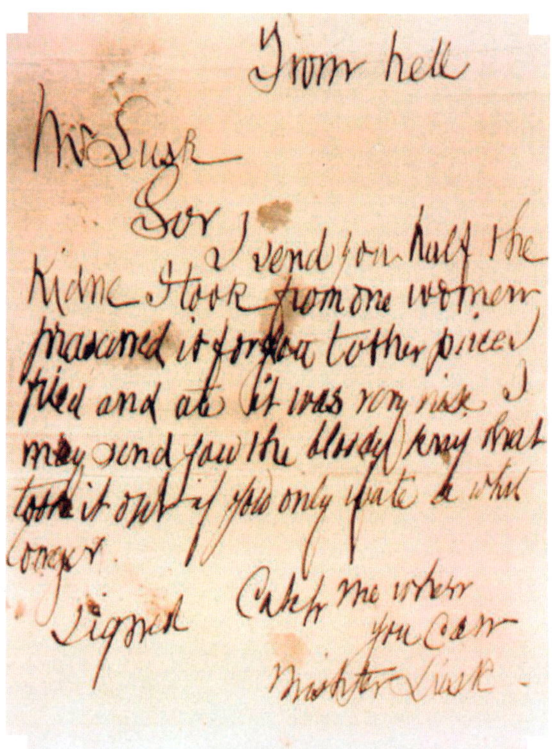

From hell

Mr Lusk
Sor
I send you half the Kidne I took from one women prasarved it for you tother piece I fried and ate it was very nise I may send you the bloody knif that took it out if you only wate a whil longer.

signed Catch me when you can Mishter Lusk

This is a photo of the original 'From Hell' letter, postmarked 15 October, 1888.

THE WORST FOR LAST

The final victim attributed to Jack the Ripper was Mary Jane Kelly, the youngest of the five at aged 25. Kelly's murder was the most horrific and took place on 9 November 1888. Unlike the other victims, who were killed outdoors, Kelly was murdered in her room at 13 Miller's Court. The scene that awaited her landlord, who discovered her body, was one of unimaginable carnage. Kelly had been completely disembowelled, her body butchered beyond recognition. Her face was slashed to the point of being unidentifiable, and her heart had been removed. The sheer brutality of the murder led many to believe that the killer had taken his time with Kelly, undisturbed as he was in the privacy of her room.

As quickly as the murders began, they ended. The killing of Mary Jane Kelly was so gruesome that some felt that the murderer had finally satiated his lust for violence. Sir Melville Macnaghten, the Assistant Commissioner of the London Metropolitan Police, had his own thoughts: 'the murderer's brain gave way altogether after his awful glut . . . and that he immediately committed suicide, or, as a possible alternative, was found to be so hopelessly mad by his relations, that he was by them confined in some asylum'.

Many theories about Jack the Ripper's identity have emerged over the years. Some suggest he was upper class, or even royalty. In contrast, others point to a surgeon, butcher or someone with anatomy knowledge due to the

Mary Jane Kelly (9 November 1888).
The final victim of the Jack the Ripper.

mutilations' precision. Prominent suspects have included Montague John Druitt, a barrister, who became a Jack the Ripper suspect due to the fact he committed his suicide shortly after the last victim's murder. Also, his alleged sightings in Whitechapel, and rumours of mental instability along with vague police statements linking a barrister to the crimes, fuelled suspicion against him. Aaron Kosminski, a Polish immigrant, became a Jack the Ripper suspect due to his proximity to the crime scenes, his known mental illness and violent behaviour towards women. In 1984, DNA evidence, taken from a blood-stained shawl allegedly left at the original murder scene, linked him to the case, although the results were controversial. Sir William Gull, Queen Victoria's own physician, came under scrutiny due to conspiracy theories suggesting a cover-up involving the royal family. Some theorists claimed he committed the murders to silence women threatening royal secrets. His medical expertise and status fuelled speculation, though there is no solid evidence. Despite extensive investigation, no conclusive evidence has ever identified the true culprit.

Jack the Ripper's crimes shocked Victorian London, both for their gruesome nature and for the killer's ability to elude capture. He preyed on the vulnerable women of Whitechapel, and his unsolved murders became a focal point of public anxiety.

ROGUES' GALLERY

Although Jack became a dreaded household name, unfortunately, he was not the only murderous monster dealing death cards to the citizens of Victorian England. However, unlike Jack, the motive behind many of these multiple murders was not psychotic blood lust but financial gain, surely a byproduct of the chaotic and desperate state of affairs in late nineteenth century London.

Mary Ann Cotton, often cited as Britain's first female serial killer, was active during the mid-nineteenth-century. She was accused of poisoning at least 21 people, including her husbands, children and stepchildren, primarily with arsenic. Cotton's alleged motive was financial gain, as she collected insurance money after the deaths of her victims. Her crimes came to light after the suspicious deaths of several family members prompted an investigation. Cotton was eventually convicted of the murder of her stepson, Charles Edward Cotton, in 1873, and was hanged later that year. Despite her conviction, some historians debate whether all the deaths attributed to her were intentional, as arsenic poisoning was common due to its wide availability and frequent use in household products at the time.

In 1862, Catherine Wilson, a British nurse, was found guilty of poisoning her patients, making her one of the most notorious female killers of the nineteenth century. Active during the 1850s and 1860s, Wilson is believed to have murdered around eight people by administering colchicum, a toxic plant-derived drug. Her victims included wealthy individuals for whom she cared and she often benefitted from her patients' wills. Wilson's knowledge of medicine helped in her choice of poison, as colchicum was difficult to detect in postmortem examinations at the time. Following the suspicious death of Mrs Maria Soames, her crimes were discovered. Wilson was sentenced to death and hanged.

Also active in the 1860s, Margaret Waters,

Suspects: First Row L–R: Seweryn Klosowski, Aaron Kosminski, Thomas Cutbush, John Pizer,James Maybrick
Second Row L–R: Sir William Withey Gull, Francis Tumblety, William Henry Bury,
Montague John Druitt, Michael Ostrog.

a notorious figure, was believed to have been responsible for the deaths of at least 19 babies and young children. In nineteenth-century Britain, 'baby farming' was a practice where families would take infants in for care in exchange for money. Waters preyed on impoverished mothers, by accepting payments in return for caring for their children. Instead she neglected and starved them, often administering opiates like laudanum to hasten their deaths. The high infant mortality rate at the time helped her evade detection until a neighbour's suspicions led to an investigation. Waters was arrested, tried and convicted of infanticide in 1870, and she was subsequently executed for her crimes.

Amelia Dyer, known as the 'Ogress of Reading', took baby farming killing to a new level and ultimately became one of Britain's most prolific baby farmer murderes and serial killers. Dyer murdered the babies, often strangling them with white tape and disposing of their bodies in rivers. Over a period of decades, she is suspected of killing hundreds of infants, though only a fraction of these deaths were officially confirmed. Dyer's crimes were uncovered in 1896 when the body of a baby was found in the Thames, leading to her arrest. She was tried and convicted of murder and subsequently hanged, becoming one of the most infamous figures in British criminal history.

The Illustrated Police News of Sunday, September 22, 1888, reporting the second victim of Jack the Ripper in Whitechapel.

The Thames Torso Murderer, an unidentified serial killer, operated in London between 1887 and 1889, contemporaneous with the infamous Jack the Ripper. The killer's modus operandi involved dismembering the bodies of victims and discarding their remains in the River Thames. Four major cases were attributed to this killer, including the Rainham Mystery, in 1887, and the Whitehall Mystery, in 1888, where parts of a woman's body were discovered in the grounds of Scotland Yard. Unlike Jack the Ripper, whose crimes targeted prostitutes in Whitechapel, this killer's identity and motive remain largely unknown, as the victims were often unidentifiable due to their gruesome dismemberment. The lack of clear forensic evidence and the distraction caused by the Ripper cases left the Thames Torso Murderer's identity a mystery.

Despite what many perceived as similarities between the Torso murders and the Ripper's, the Metropolitan Police claimed the modus operandi was different: 'the victims of Jack the Ripper suffered progressive abdominal- and genital-area mutilation, whereas the Thames Torso Murderer dismembered the bodies of his victims'.

George Chapman, born Seweryn Kłosowski, was a Polish-born barber and serial killer who poisoned three of his mistresses between 1897 and 1902. His cold and calculated murders earned him the nickname the 'Borough Poisoner'. Chapman's notoriety extends beyond these murders, as he is considered by some as a potential suspect in the Jack the Ripper case. Chapman lived in Whitechapel during the Ripper murders, and his violent tendencies and close proximity to the crimes fuelled speculation. However, no conclusive evidence linked him to the Ripper killings. He was arrested in 1902, convicted of poisoning and hanged in 1903.

THE RIPPER REIMAGINED

Though Jack the Ripper vanished into the fog of Victorian London, the mystery of his identity continues to evolve well into the 21st century. Advances in forensic science, digital archiving, and a fervent community of "Ripperologists" have breathed new life into a case that remains officially unsolved over 130 years later.

Perhaps the most headline-grabbing development came in 2014, when author Russell Edwards claimed to have solved the case using DNA analysis. A shawl allegedly found near victim Catherine Eddowes was tested, and mitochondrial DNA was matched to Aaron Kosminski, a Polish barber and one of the prime suspects in the original investigation. While the media touted this as a breakthrough, many experts criticized the methodology, pointing to contamination risks and the limitations of mitochondrial DNA, which cannot confirm a single individual.

Digital reconstructions of crime scenes, geographic profiling, and AI-assisted analysis of historical documents have since added nuance rather than certainty. Other suspects—Montague John Druitt, Sir William Gull, and even painter Walter Sickert—remain in circulation, each bolstered by new spins on old evidence.

Online forums, podcasts, and documentaries continue to dissect every letter, map, and photograph. The Ripper has become less a man and more a cultural mirror: reflecting fears of urban anonymity, class divides, and the failure of modern institutions to guarantee safety or justice. While science may one day identify the killer, the myth of Jack the Ripper has already outlived the man—if he ever existed as a single person at all.

H.H. HOLMES – COMPLEX KILLER OR SIMPLE FRAUDSTER?

Across the Atlantic, in the 1800s Americans also had their fair share of murderous maniacs. A man not as well-known as Jack the Ripper, H.H. Holmes was allegedly as brutal and, according to Holmes himself, an even more prolific killer. Often described as America's first serial killer, Holmes, also known as Dr Henry Howard Holmes and Herman Webster Mudgett, built a life of deception long before he was connected to a series of murders in Chicago. In 1883, as a medical student at the University of Michigan, Holmes first started engaging in schemes to defraud insurance companies. One of his initial scams involved stealing cadavers from the university's anatomy labs and disfiguring them to stage fake accidents. Holmes would then claim the bodies were those of people who he had taken out life insurance policies, collecting the payout as the beneficiary.

Herman Webster Mudgett (1861–96). The world came to know him as H.H. Holmes.

In the 1880s, Holmes moved to Chicago, where he became involved in real estate; he opened a drugstore. Its success enabled Holmes to buy property across the street and construct the now-infamous three-story building that would come to be known as his 'Murder Castle'. Holmes' fraudulent activities flourished during the building's construction. He hired and fired multiple contractors without paying them, frequently claiming their work was unsatisfactory. This tactic enabled him to keep the construction process in constant flux, which some say was to conceal the hidden rooms, trapdoors and secret passages he was installing for more nefarious purposes.

Holmes was adept at assuming false identities and weaving intricate webs of deception. One of his most common scams involved wooing wealthy women, marrying them and stealing their fortunes before disappearing. He married several women at the same time, using different aliases for each marriage. His wives, Clara Lovering, Myrta Belknap and Georgiana Yoke, were all unaware of each other.

The marriages were part of a larger pattern of swindling. Holmes often involved business partners in elaborate schemes, only to betray them. For example, he convinced Benjamin Pitezel, a fellow scam artist, to join him in an insurance fraud scheme in which Pitezel would fake his own death. However, instead Holmes murdered Pitezel. His undoing began with this murder and the subsequent disappearance of Pitezel's children. He reportedly killed three while keeping up the pretence that they were still alive. Philadelphia authorities became suspicious of Holmes, and a detective, Frank Geyer, launched an investigation into his activities. Geyer tracked Holmes's movements and discovered the bodies of the Pitezel children along the way. At the same time, insurers were growing suspicious of Holmes's numerous claims.

On 17 November 1894, Holmes was arrested at an apartment on 838 Columbus Avenue in Scollay Square by Boston police officers and a Pinkerton detective agency agent. He was being held on a warrant for horse theft in Texas, and police suspected he was trying to flee the country with his third wife. While in custody, the police were granted a search warrant for the building at W 63rd Street. Accounts differ on the amount of human remains found in the basement, but investigators did discover among them what is believed to have been those of Benjamin Pitezel.

Holmes was charged with conspiracy to defraud the Fidelity Mutual Life Insurance Company and convicted of murdering Benjamin Pitezel. He was sentenced to death and executed by hanging at Moyamensing Prison on 7 May 1896.

The execution of H.H. Holmes, Philadelphia Moyamensing Prison, 1896.

BODY COUNT

How many people did Holmes kill? Well, that depends on who you ask. The tabloids tend to report a body count upwards of 200. Holmes himself initially confessed to 27, but during his trial, he told his lawyer he had killed 133. The court system believed the actual number was nine. However, he was only convicted on one count of murder – that of his business partner, Benjamin Pitezel.

Despite that fact, based on the evidence, the nine murders seem like a more realistic number. They are:

JULIA AND PEARL CONNER (1891)

Julia was the wife of one of Holmes's employees who worked in his building. After having an affair with Holmes, Julia and her daughter, Pearl, disappeared. Their bodies were never recovered, but it is generally believed that Holmes killed them.

EMELINE CIGRAND (1892)

Holmes hired Emeline as a secretary and proposed marriage to her. She disappeared soon after, and it's believed Holmes killed her in his specially constructed airtight vault.

MINNIE WILLIAMS (1893)

Minnie was a wealthy woman Holmes lured to his hotel, intending to steal her inheritance. She disappeared after signing over her property to him. It is widely accepted that Holmes killed her, though her body was never found.

NANNIE WILLIAMS (1893)

Minnie's sister, Nannie, also disappeared shortly after meeting Holmes, and she is presumed to have been murdered.

BENJAMIN PITEZEL (1894)

Holmes' most well-documented murder involved his business associate, Benjamin Pitezel as part of a life insurance scam. Holmes claims he soaked Pitezel's body in benzene and burnt Pitezel while he was alive, but after knocking him unconscious with chloroform.

ALICE, NELLIE, AND HOWARD PITEZEL (1894)

Holmes also murdered Pitezel's children – Alice, Nellie and Howard. He killed them after convincing their mother, Carrie Pitezel, that he was taking them to meet their father, who was already dead. Ten-year-old Howard was killed in Indianapolis via poisoning. Fifteen days later, Holmes confined the two girls, Alice and Nellie, in a trunk and asphyxiated them with gas.

How many people did Holmes kill? [...] The tabloids tend to report a body count upwards of 200.

THE MURDER CASTLE

The only information more controversial than the number of murders committed by Holmes is the building he constructed at 611 W 63rd Street in Chicago, Illinois. Rather than just a pharmacy storefront with multiple apartments above was it a Murder Castle complete with a torture room, trap doors, a corpse chute, a maze of secret hallways, false floors and soundproof rooms outfitted with vents through which he'd send poison gas to asphyxiate his guests and a furnace in the basement to dispose of the dead bodies?

If you adhere to the reporting in the local papers of the day, a lead story on H.H. Holmes and his Murder Castle would read something like this: The construction of the Murder Castle was meticulously designed by Holmes himself, frequently hiring and firing workers to ensure no one would understand the building's true purpose. The interior of the building was a maze of secret passageways, trap doors and soundproof rooms. Corridors led to dead ends, and some doors opened to brick walls. Many rooms were equipped with gas jets that Holmes could activate to suffocate his victims. The hotel even had a greased chute that

HOLMES' "CASTLE" (*63d St, Chicago, Ill.*)

Exterior view of residence of Herman Webster Mudgett, a.k.a. H.H. Holmes, on 63rd Street. Mudgett's home was named the Murder Castle.

To-Day

The Journal shows one of its best and greatest issues—a tri-directive of past promises and a new promise for the future—the greatest Sunday paper, for Three cents.

THE JOURNAL

To-Morrow

NO. 4,896. NEW YORK, SUNDAY, APRIL 12, 1896.—14 PAGES.—COPYRIGHT, 1896, BY W. R. HEARST. PRICE THREE CENTS.

FULL CONFESSION OF H. H. HOLMES.

(Made to the Journal by the Condemned Man----The Only Authentic Statement of His Crimes.)

Most Appalling Record of Murder to Which Any Man Has Ever Affixed His Signature.

He Analyzes His Sentiments and Describes His Feelings While Doing Away with More Than a Score of Victims.

TORTURING HELPLESS MEN, WOMEN AND CHILDREN TO DEATH.

Some Died Easily from Suffocation or Poison, but Others Were Starved in the Secret Rooms of the Castle or Choked with Gas---Pitezel Was Burned Alive---A Pen Picture of the Multi-Murderer by Himself---He Says His Face and Body Have Taken on the Look of Satan and Treats Himself as a Psychological Phenomenon.

This is the story of a monster; a record of crime that will make a chapter in future histories as important as anything recorded by historians of civilization and morals.

Written by the perpetrator himself while he waits for the summons to mount the gallows, it has a value apart from that pertaining to the ends of justice. In the commission of more than a dozen murders, this fiend has managed to violate almost every law of man or God. Originally he was merely a murderer for the incidental profit, but soon he began to look upon murder as simply an incident in combatting the ordinary difficulties of life. He killed a woman because he was tired of her, or because he feared that her interest in another man would deprive him of that man's services. He found a man who had insured his life in favor of one of his victims; he killed the man to gather the insurance for himself.

The third stage of his iniquity was murdering for the mere pleasure of seeing his victim die, and the grotesque horror of his murders is beyond belief. One man he made drunk, and while he had him helpless he bound him and burned him alive, though many easier and safer methods of bringing about his death were open to him. Another man he enticed into a furnace and turned the consuming heat on with as little compunction as if it had been the most ordinary of chemical experiments. He built a vault to make murder easier; he smothered children in trunks, merely to get them out of the way. He actually adopted murder as a profession in life and hesitated at nothing in the carrying on of his business. He never calculated on the possibility of being discovered, but thought to pursue his horrid occupation as long as the passion for blood lasted, or it would profit him to kill.

This is the story as it came from his own pen; there is no remorse in it. He tells of murders that no one knew were murders. He admits his guilt of every one of the crimes of which he was suspected.

He has even grown interested in the psychological study of his own motives, and the picture he has drawn of himself could gain nothing by fine writing or strong adjectives. He is a horror such as you read of in the pages of an alienist writer dealing with mental monsters of the Middle Ages. There is no danger that he will find imitators. A man born with the mental and moral twist of Holmes is a freak of nature as much as a four-armed woman or an elephant-headed boy. His purpose in telling the story is not born of any saving feeling of horror or repentance.

HOLMES'S OWN STORY.

The Narrative in Full Exactly as Written by the Condemned Man.

H. H. HOLMES, THE ARCH CRIMINAL OF MODERN HISTORY.

From the latest photograph of the murderer. A flashlight taken in jail for the Journal.

To the New York Journal
I positively & emphatically deny the assertions that any confession has been made by me Except one & which is the only one that will be made. The original confession is the one given to the New York Journal. It alone is genuine all others are untrue
April 11th 1896 Signed H. H. Holmes

POLICE PHOTOGRAPHS OF HOLMES TAKEN SHORTLY AFTER HIS ARREST.

The *New York Journal* of Sunday 12 April 1896, ran an exposé that was reported to be H.H. Holmes confessing to all his heinous acts and revealing his victim's identities.

allowed Holmes to swiftly dispose of bodies in the basement.

Once inside the Murder Castle, Holmes subjected his victims to unimaginable horrors. His methods of torture and murder were varied, ranging from asphyxiation in airtight vaults to poisoning. Some victims were starved or left to die of thirst in locked rooms, while others were strapped to a surgical table where Holmes would dissect them alive. He showed no mercy, taking a sick pleasure in experimenting with different methods of killing.

The disposal of his victims was equally gruesome. Holmes often sold their skeletons to medical schools, taking advantage of the demand for anatomical specimens in the medical community. The basement of the Murder Castle was a veritable chamber of horrors, where Holmes would strip the flesh from the bodies, dissolve them in acid vats or burn them in a furnace. He also experimented with surgical tools, and some reports suggest that he inserted straight pins into the bodies of his victims, including the sensitive areas of the groin, such as the taint, demonstrating a perverse fascination with inflicting as much pain as possible.

The jury is still out though, and rabid debates still rage about who presented the most accurate accounts of what happened inside the Murder Castle. However, a few things are for sure, and that is Herman Webster Mudgett was a sociopath, a pathological liar, a narcissist and an intelligent lifelong conman who murdered for profit or convenience.

England and the United States of the Victorian-era were beset by a dark undercurrent that lurked beneath their veneer of civility. The era's fascination with death and the macabre was mirrored by a surge of sinister figures who preyed upon the unsuspecting. Streets that bustled by day transformed into hunting grounds for serial killers by night.

Meanwhile, swindlers and conmen wove intricate webs of deceit, exploiting the era's rapid urbanization to slip through the cracks of nascent police forces. Even the concept of the 'angel in the house' was subverted as some women, like the infamous Mary Ann Cotton, embraced murder to escape their domestic confines.

This was an age of contradictions, where technological progress clashed with an ever-present shadow of human depravity. But unfortunately the turn of the century brought more than a new dawn; it ushered in even greater unrest. What followed in the early 1920s was a world forever changed by the Great War's horrors, where the moral certainties of the Victorian age shattered. Europe and America would soon find themselves grappling not just with ghosts of the past, but with new terrors born not from cobblestone alleys but from the trenches, the trauma and the relentless march of modernization. ❀

The cover of the book *Holmes Own Story*. A dark and chilling narrative from the pen of Dr. H. H. Holmes.

CHAPTER XIII

The QUEEN'S LAST BREATH

A MONARCH'S FAREWELL

THE BEGINNING OF THE END

The final days of Queen Victoria, who passed away on 22 January 1901, were shrouded in the weight of a country losing a monarch who had an extended and significant reign. At the time of her death, she had ruled Britain, and a great deal of the world, for over 63 years, the longest reign of any British monarch until that point. Her longevity had solidified her as a monumental figure not just in British history but globally, too. The Victorian Era was a time of dramatic industrial, cultural, political and scientific change and innovation, led by a vibrant queen. But in the final days of her life, the woman who had come to symbolize an entire era was a frail woman in her eighties, who had experienced much personal loss, suffering from physical and mental decline.

In December 1900, Queen Victoria's health began to rapidly deteriorate. She had been experiencing increasing mobility issues due to arthritis, and her eyesight had been failing, making even the simple pleasures of reading and writing difficult for her. She complained of weakness and loss of appetite, symptoms which her physicians struggled to diagnose. By the beginning of January 1901, her family, including her children and grandchildren, were summoned to Osborne House on the Isle of Wight, where the queen had retreated to spend her final days. The royal family knew the end was near.

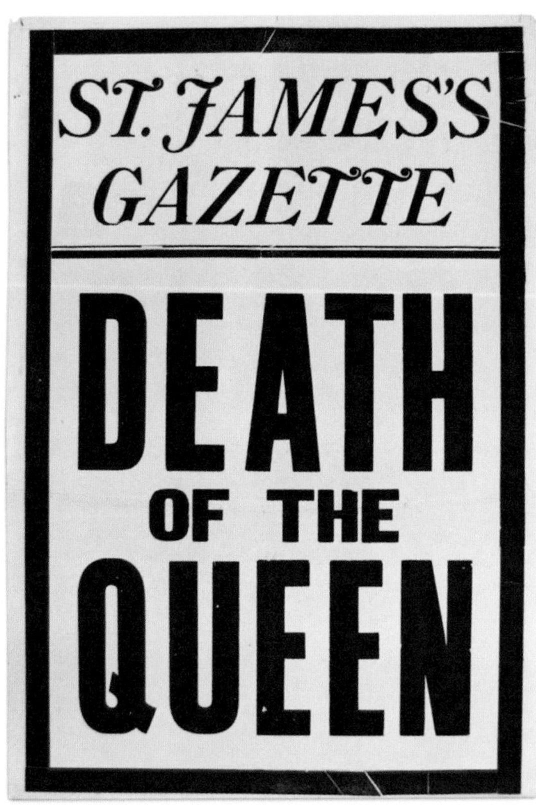

A newsstand banner from the St. James's Gazette announcing the death of Queen Victoria.

While the queen had never truly recovered from the death of her beloved husband, Prince Albert, in 1861, the last weeks of her life were marked by visible emotional and physical exhaustion. She spoke less frequently and had a distant, pained look that concerned those around her. The queen had often referred to herself as ready to join her beloved Albert, expressing a longing to reunite with him in the afterlife.

THE DEATH OF A QUEEN

On 22 January 1901, Queen Victoria died peacefully at Osborne House. She was surrounded by her family, including her son, the Prince of Wales (the soon to be King Edward VII), and her grandson, Kaiser Wilhelm II of Germany. Her passing marked the end of the Victorian Era and symbolized the closing of a historical chapter that had seen the British Empire rise to its height of power.

At the time of her death, Victoria was the figurehead of a global empire, but she was also an intensely private person who had spent much of her later life in mourning for her beloved husband. Her death was not a sudden event, as her family and the nation had been prepared for the possibility of losing its queen after weeks of reports about her ailing health.

As news of her death spread, the British Empire went into mourning . . . again. Although Victoria had become a distant figure to many of her subjects in her later years, her death was felt deeply across Britain and the world.

The coffin of Queen Victoria being carried into St George's Chapel in Windsor Castle.

A FUNERAL IN WHITE

Queen Victoria's funeral was a grand event befitting her long and illustrious reign. It took place on 2 February 1901 and was notable for its adherence to the traditions that Victoria herself had meticulously planned. One of her most significant wishes was that her funeral should not be a state occasion in the grand ceremonial style that had marked royal funerals in the past. Victoria, though the queen of an empire, wanted her funeral to reflect the simpler aspects of her life.

She requested that she be laid to rest beside her beloved Albert in the Frogmore Mausoleum in Windsor, where he was buried. Victoria maintained a deeply personal mourning for Albert throughout her life, and this final request ensured that her death would be linked, symbolically, to the husband for whom she had never stopped grieving.

Her body was transported from the Isle of Wight to Windsor, where a procession carried her to the mausoleum. The funeral, deeply rooted in tradition, was also marked by the military honours that befitted the monarch of the British Empire. Tens of thousands of mourners lined the streets, and the presence of royalty and dignitaries from across Europe underscored Victoria's importance on the global stage.

Perhaps, most notably, her coffin was draped in white rather than black. This was her final defiance against the overwhelming culture of mourning she had come to symbolize during her reign. Although she spent so much of her life in black mourning clothes, Victoria's final procession, in white, signalled for her the end of an era of grief.

Tens of thousands of mourners lined the streets, and the presence of royalty and dignitaries from across Europe underscored Victoria's importance on the global stage.

Queen Victoria's train engine, the Royal-Sovereign, was used to transport the coffin and the royal mourners from Paddington to Frogmore mausoleum at Windsor Castle.

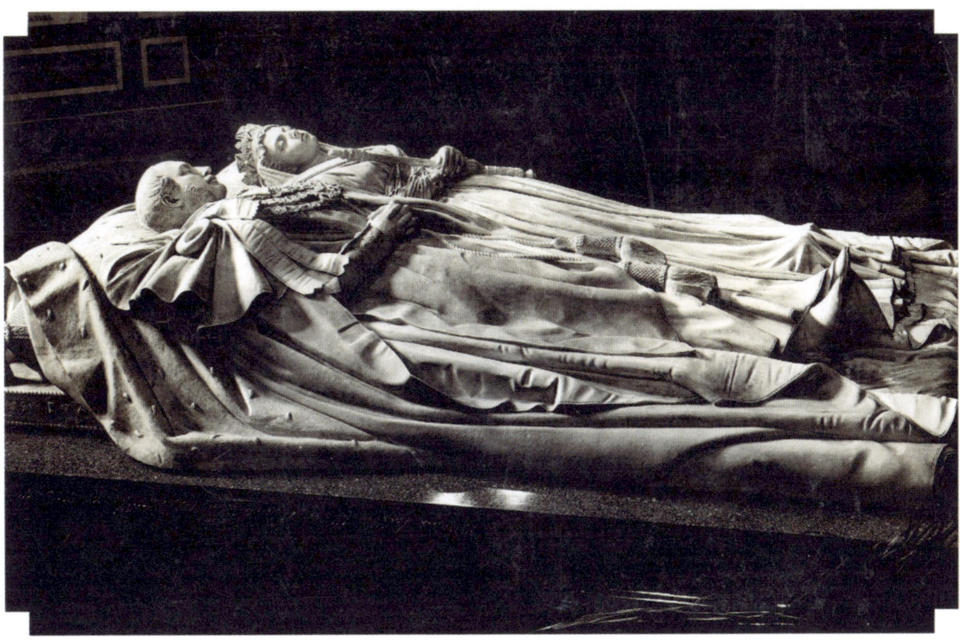

The elaborate tomb of the Royal couple, each depicted in recumbent effigies in marble sculpted by the Italian sculptor Carlo Marochetti.

THE WORLD'S REACTION

For many, her death signalled the end of not just an era but a way of life. Victorian values – marked by strict social mores, industrial advancement, and imperial expansion – were deeply associated with the Queen herself. Her passing sparked a profound sense of reflection across the empire.

The death of Queen Victoria had great significance internationally. Royal families across Europe, many of whom were related to her by blood, expressed their sorrow. Kaiser Wilhelm II, her grandson, was deeply affected by her death, as were other monarchs who viewed Victoria as a familial and political figurehead.

In the United States, where Victoria was held in high esteem, her death was met with genuine sadness. Though the American Revolution had severed direct ties to the British monarchy, Queen Victoria's reign had coincided with a time of friendship between the two nations. Across the world, Victoria had symbolized continuity and stability.

THE EVENING JOURNAL'S CIRCULATION IS GREATER ALL THE OTHER NEWSPAPERS

THE 20TH CENTURY NEWSPAPER

NEW YORK JOURNAL

W. R. HEARST

QUEEN EXTRA

TUESDAY. TUESDAY. PRICE ONE CENT.

QUEEN VICTORIA DEAD

Aged Monarch Passed Out of Life Without a Struggle as if Going Asleep.

HER MAJESTY, QUEEN VICTORIA.

Front page news of the *New York Journal*, ran the news of Queen Victoria's death as an 'EXTRA'!

THE PALL OF SORROW IS LIFTED

For many years following the death of Prince Albert in 1861, Queen Victoria embraced mourning as a central part of her public and private identity. This deep mourning affected the entire nation. Victoria's fixation on mourning set a tone of solemnity and sorrow that permeated British culture. Mourning, in a sense, became institutionalized, with elaborate rituals, public expectations and strict guidelines on how grief should be publicly displayed.

However, with the queen's demise in 1901, there was a palpable shift in the national psyche. The new king, Edward VII, signalled a break from the past. Known for his more cosmopolitan and sociable nature, Edward brought a lighter tone to the monarchy and to British society. The Edwardian era was marked by a focus on modernity, fashion and new forms of entertainment, shedding much of the Victorian stiffness and morbidity. The dawn of the twentieth century brought with it a sense of renewal and optimism as Britain began to look forward rather than dwell on the past.

Our journey through the shadows of Victorian-era Europe and the United States has taken us through a world steeped in the ever-present reality of death. For the people of that time, death was not merely a distant inevitability but an intimate, relentless companion. With lifespans cut cruelly short by a litany of issues, the Victorian obsession with mourning was not born of morbid curiosity. Rather, it was a cultural response to an existence defined by uncertainty and loss.

In a society where nearly every family had felt the searing pain of a child's death, where consumption (tuberculosis) claimed lives in droves, and where smallpox swept through communities like a grim reaper's hand, mourning became a form of expression, a language through which grief could be made tangible.

Yet, despite – or perhaps because of – this constant brush with mortality, the Victorians found ways to make meaning out of their suffering. Mourning customs, laden with symbolism and ritual, offered solace and structure in times of profound despair and transformed death into something both deeply personal and universally shared.

But it was also a time of contradiction. As society made death visible, it also sought to contain it, to fence it within the boundaries of decorum and propriety. The Victorians were as obsessed with hiding the true face of death as they were with honouring it. Coffins lined with plush interiors, elaborate gravestones and euphemistic language all served to obscure the harsh reality of decay. In trying to make death beautiful, they revealed a fear not just of dying, but of being forgotten, of vanishing into the void without a trace.

In the end, what remains of the Victorian fascination with death is a reminder of our own fragility. It is a testament to how, even in the face of despair, humanity seeks to create meaning, to find beauty and to hold on to the memory of those who have gone beyond the veil. ❀

Endnotes

CHAPTER I – THRONES AND BONES: THE GRIEF THAT GOVERNS

1. Clara Rising, *The Taylor File: The Mysterious Death of a President*, First Edition: Xlibris, 2007.

CHAPTER II – IN THE SHADOW OF THE SCYTHE: LIFE AND DEATH IN THE VICTORIAN ERA

2. Sheila M. Rothman, *Living in the Shadow of Death: Tuberculosis and the Social Experience of Illness in American History* New York, NY: BasicBooks, 1994, p.190.

3. TB 101 for Healthcare Workers, Centers for Disease Control and Prevention, https://www.cdc.gov/tb/webcourses/tb101/page2621.html

4. Judith Flanders, *Inside the Victorian Home: A Portrait of Domestic Life in Victorian England*, New York, NY: W.W. Norton, 2004.

5. How has life expectancy changed over time?, Decennial Life Tables, ONS, https://www.ons.gov.uk/

6. T.H. Tulchinsky, (2018). John Snow, Cholera, the Broad Street Pump; Waterborne Diseases Then and Now. *Case Studies in Public Health*, 77. https://doi.org/10.1016/B978-0-12-804571-8.00017-2

7. David M. Oshinsky, *Bellevue: Three Centuries of Medicine and Mayhem at America's Most Storied Hospital*, New York, NY: Anchor Books, 2017, p.68.

CHAPTER IV – BRUSHES WITH MORTALITY: VICTORIAN ART IN THE SHADOW OF DEATH

8. John Frith, 'History of Tuberculosis. Part 1 – Phthisis, consumption and the White Plague', *JMVH*, Vol. 22, No. 2.

9. Caroline, Seabury, *The Diary of Caroline Seabury, 1854–1863*, edited by Suzanne L. Bunkers, Madison, WI: The University of Wisconsin Press, 1991.

10. R. Dubos and J. Dubos, *Tuberculosis, Man, and Society. The White Plague*, Boston, MA: Little, Brown, and Company, 1952.

CHAPTER V – CITY OF THE DEAD: FAMILY PLOTS TO THE NECROPOLIS

11. UK Public General Acts, 65 (Regnal. 10_and_11_Vict), 1847.

12. 'Coping with Cholera. How did the authorities react in 19th century?', The National Archives, https://www.nationalarchives.gov.uk/education/resources/coping-with-cholera/

13. *Execution*, published broadside, probable date published: shelfmark: L.C.Fol.74(097), 1829.

14. S. Tarlow, Curious afterlives: the enduring appeal of the criminal corpse. *Mortality* (Abingdon), 2016 Jul 2;21(3):210-228. doi: 10.1080/13576275.2016.1181328. Epub 2016 Jun 1. PMID: 27366110; PMCID: PMC4917903.

15. Edward Halperin. 'The Poor, the Black, and the Marginalized as the Source of Cadavers in United States Anatomical Education', *Clinical Anatomy* Vol. 20, No. 5, 2007, 489-495.

16. Marilyn Manson/Twiggy Ramirez, 'The Beautiful People', *Antichrist Superstar*, Interscope Records, 1996.

17. C.M. Milroy, A Brief History of the Literature on Postmortem Changes to the 19th Century, Acad Forensic Pathol. 2016 Mar;6(1):2-11. doi: 10.23907/2016.001. Epub 2016 Mar 1. PMID: 31239868; PMCID: PMC6474507.

CHAPTER VI – CROSSING OVER: COMMUNICATING WITH THE GREAT BEYOND

18. Online atlas explores north–south divide in childbirth and child mortality during Victorian era, University of Cambridge, 15 May 2018, https://www.cam.ac.uk/research

CHAPTER VII – THE DARK ARTS: A DANCE WITH DEATH IN LITERATURE AND CULTURE

19. Proteus syndrome causes an overgrowth of skin, bones, muscles, fatty tissues and blood and lymphatic vessels. It is a progressive condition wherein children are usually born without any obvious deformities.

20. Neurofibromatosis 1 (NF1), historically called von Recklinghausen's disease, is a genetic disorder characterized by increased risk of developing non-cancerous (benign) and cancerous (malignant) tumours, as well as various other physical and neurological manifestations.

CHAPTER VIII – MEMENTO MORI: KEEPSAKES OF THE DEAD

21. William Shakespeare, *Henry V*, Act 3, Scene 3.

CHAPTER IX – THE HOUSE OF SHADOWS: FROM HOME TO FUNERAL HOME

22. 'Cream of Current Literature', *Dundee Evening Telegraph*, 10 May 1877: p.4.

23. Ibid.

24. Ibid.

CHAPTER X – SHOOTING THE DEAD: A FINAL FOCUS

25. George Bradford(e), 'Odd Jobs No. 10. A Grave Subject', *Photographic News*, 7 July 1882, pp.394–5.

26. N. Bown, 'Empty Hands and Precious Pictures: Post-mortem Portrait Photographs of Children', *Australasian Journal of Victorian Studies*, Vol 14, No.2, 2010, pp.8–24.

CHAPTER XI – TOIL AND TRAGEDY: WORKING YOURSELF TO DEATH

27. E.P. Thompson. *The Making of the English Working Class*, New York, NY: Vintage Books, 1966.

28. Richard M. and Robert B. Sherman, music and lyrics, '*Chim Chim Cher-ee*', *Mary Poppins (original soundtrack)*, Walt Disney, 1964.

29. Henry Mayhew, London Labour and the London Poor, Vol. 3, *The Morning Chronicle*, 1851.

Picture credits

p.2 courtesy of Heritage Image Partnership Ltd/Alamy; p.6 courtesy of Pictorial Press Ltd/Alamy; p.9 above courtesy of Heritage Image Partnership Ltd/Alamy; p.9 below above courtesy of Chronicle/Alamy; p.10 courtesy of World History Archive/Alamy; p.11 courtesy of Pictorial Press Ltd/Alamy; p.13 courtesy of Contraband Collection/Alamy; p.14 courtesy of Carlo Bollo/Alamy; p.17 courtesy of Pictures Now/Alamy; p.18 courtesy of North Wind Picture Archives/Alamy; p.19 courtesy of North Wind Picture Archives/Alamy; p.20 courtesy of FLHC FBDB4/Alamy; p.22 above courtesy of Chronicle/Alamy; p.23 courtesy of The Picture Art Collection/Alamy; p.24 courtesy of Zoom Historical/Alamy; p.25 courtesy of ART Collection/Alamy; p.26 courtesy of Well/BOT/ Alamy; p.29 courtesy of Niday Picture Library/ Alamy; p.30 courtesy of Bettmann/Getty; p.31 courtesy of Niday Picture Library/Alamy; p.34 courtesy of Bettmann/Getty; p.35, courtesy of DappledHistory.com/Alamy; p.36 courtesy of Moon of Pearl; p.39, courtesy of Science History Images/Alamy; p.41 courtesy of mikroman6/ Getty; p.44 courtesy of GL Archive/ Alamy; p.46 courtesy of Colin Waters/Alamy; p.47 courtesy of Moon of Pearl; p.48 courtesy of The History Emporium/Alamy; p.50 courtesy of Florilegius/ Alamy; p.51 courtesy of Classic Photographics/ Alamy; p.52 courtesy of Moon of Pearl; p.53 courtesy of Kirn Vintage Stock/Getty; p.54 courtesy of Heritage Images/Getty; p.55 courtesy of Amoret Tanner/Alamy; p.56 above courtesy of Chronicle/Alamy; p.59 courtesy of Lebrecht Music & Arts/Alamy; p.60 courtesy of The Artchives/Alamy; p.61 courtesy of ARTGEN/ Alamy; p.62 courtesy of IanDagnall Computing/ Alamy; p.63 courtesy of IanDagnall Computing/ Alamy; p.64 courtesy of Peter Barritt/Alamy; p.65 courtesy of IanDagnall Computing/Alamy; p.66 Artepics/Alamy; p.67 coutesy of The Picture Art Collection/Alamy; p.68 courtesy of Pictures Now/Alamy; p.73 courtesy of Bettmann/ Getty; p.74 courtesy of Simon Price/Alamy; p.76 courtesy of Dan Howell Photography; p.78 courtesy of Arcaid Images/Alamy; p.80 courtesy of The Library of Congress; p.84 courtesy of ART Collection/Alamy; p.85 above courtesy of The Print Collector/Alamy, below American Photo Archive/Alamy; p.86 courtesy of History and Art Collection/Alamy; p.89 ; p.91 courtesy of Heritage Image Partnership Ltd/Alamy; p.95 courtesy of Shawshots/Alamy; p.93 courtesy of The Library of Congress; p.96 courtesy of The Library of Congress; p.97 courtesy of Jimlop collection/Alamy; p.98 courtesy of Smith Archive/Alamy; p.99 courtesy of Gainew Gallery/ Alamy; p.100 courtesy of World History Archive/ Alamy; p.102 courtesy of World History Archive/ Alamy; p.103 courtesy of Old Paper Studios/ Alamy; p.104 courtesy of cineclassico/Alamy; p.105 courtesy of Pictorial Press Ltd/Alamy;

p.106 courtesy of IanDagnall Computing/Alamy; p.107 courtesy of Digital Image Library/Alamy; p.109 courtesy of Archive Pics/Alamy; p.110 courtesy of IanDagnall Computing/Alamy; p.111 Science History Images/Alamy; p.112 courtesy of Lebrecht Music & Arts/Alamy; p.114, courtesy of INTERFOTO/Alamy; p.116 courtesy of Portis Imaging/Alamy; p.118 courtesy of AF Fotografie/Alamy; p.121 courtesy of Heritage Image Partnership Ltd/Alamy; p.123 courtesy of Moon of Pearl; p.125 adam eastland/Alamy; p.126 courtesy of Heritage Image Partnership Ltd/Alamy; p.127 courtesy of INTERFOTO/Alamy; p.128 Science History Images/Alamy; p.131 courtesy of Dave Bagnall Collection/Alamy; p.132 courtesy of Moon of Pearl; p.133 courtesy of Paul Popper/Popperfoto/Getty; p.135 courtesy of Wellcome Collection; p.137 courtesy of FLHC FBDB4/Alamy; p.139 courtesy of Science History Images/Alamy; p.140 courtesy of Heritage Image Partnership Ltd/Alamy; p.142 courtesy of Darling Archive/Alamy; p.143 courtesy of The Library of Congress; p.146 courtesy of Moon of Pearl; p.147 courtesy of Clements Library; p.148 courtesy of Clements Library; p.149 courtesy of UtCon Collection/Alamy; p.151 courtesy of Clements Library; p.154 courtesy of Clements Library; p.156 Stocktrek Images, Inc./Alamy; p.158 IanDagnall Computing/Alamy; p.159 courtesy of Walker Art Library/Alamy; p.160 courtesy of 19th era/Alamy; p.161 courtesy of World History Archive/Alamy; p.162 courtesy of Science History Images/Alamy; p.164 courtesy of Heritage Image Partnership Ltd/Alamy; p.165 courtesy of Everett Collection Historical/Alamy; p.166 courtesy of Hulton Archive/Getty; p.167 courtesy of adoc-photos/Getty; p.168 courtesy of Historic Images/Alamy; p.170 courtesy of Axis Images/Alamy; p.171 courtesy of Express Newspapers/Getty; p.172 courtesy of The Picture Art Collection/Alamy; p.173 courtesy of World History Archive/Alamy; p.174 courtesy of The Picture Art Collection/Alamy; p.175 courtesy of World History Archive/Alamy; p.177 courtesy of Maurice Savage/Alamy; p.178 courtesy of Lordprice Collection/Alamy; p.180 courtesy of GL Archive/Alamy; p.181 courtesy of Signal Photos/Alamy; p.183 courtesy of Chicago History Museum/Alamy; p.184 courtesy of The Library of Congress; p.185 courtesy of The Library of Congress; p.186 courtesy of Recall Pictures/Alamy; p.188 courtesy of History and Art Collection/Alamy; p.189 courtesy of Historical Images Archive/Alamy; p.191 above courtesy of Chronicle/Alamy; p.191 below courtesy of Sueddeutsche Zeitung Photo/Alamy; p.192 courtesy of John Frost Newspapers/Alamy; p.202 courtesy of Bettmann/Getty; p.204 courtesy of North Wind Picture Archives/Alamy.

Index

Page numbers in *italics* indicate illustration captions.

TAINTED
MEAT
&
FISH
IMPURE

Acknowledgements

My sincere thanks to Lee Sobel, my dedicated agent, for his belief in this project from the start. To my wife, Martine, and my son, Anthony - your love and support are the heartbeat behind everything I do. A sincere thank you to John Parton, Senior Commissioning Editor and Charlotte Frost, Senior Editor at Quarto for your guidance and trust. I'm also deeply grateful to Masumi Briozzo, whose keen eye as Designer helped bring the visuals to life. And to everyone at Quarto who lent their time, talent, and care - this book wouldn't exist without you.

About the Author

US-based Paul Gambino has been an avid collector of the bizarre for over 20 years with an extensive collection of Victorian memorial photographs, antique funeria, mug shots, and vintage religious items (including a life-sized St. Sebastian and Virgin Mary salvaged from a 19th-century church in Pennsylvania).

His previous books include *Morbid Curiosities* (2016), *Skulls* (2021) and *Killer Collections* (2022).

Quarto

First published in 2025 by Frances Lincoln
an imprint of The Quarto Group.
One Triptych Place, London, SE1 9SH
United Kingdom
T (0)20 7700 9000
www.Quarto.com

EEA Representation, WTS Tax d.o.o., Žanova ulica 3,
4000 Kranj, Slovenia www.wts-tax.si

A catalogue record for this book is available from the British Library.

ISBN 978-1-83600-422-6
EBOOK ISBN 978-1-83600-423-3

10 9 8 7 6 5 4 3 2 1

Book Designer: Masumi Briozzo
Publisher: Philip Cooper
Senior Commissioning Editor: John Parton
Senior Designer: Isabel Eeles
Senior Editor: Charlotte Frost
Senior Production Manager: Rohana Yusof

Printed in Guangdong, China TT062025